A History of ROSEDALE

The Story of Yorkshire's most Beautiful Dale

by

Raymond H. Hayes, M.B.E., F.S.A.

Foreword and General Introduction
by
W.J.L. Young

Design: Julie A. Gow; National Park Department
First edition 1971 Second Edition 1973 Third Edition and Revision 1985
Reprinted 1987

ISBN 0 907480 10 1

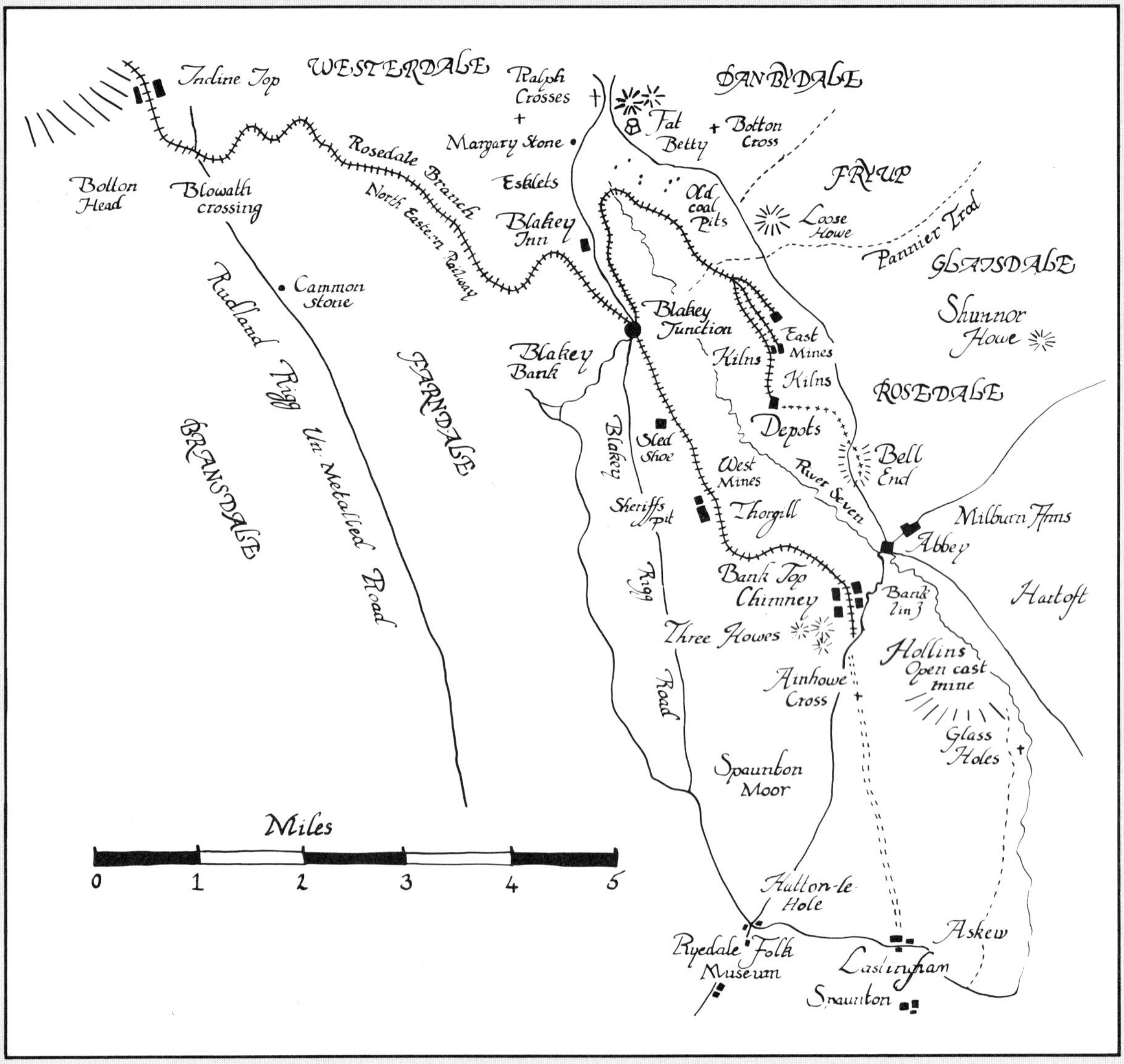

Incline Top
WESTERDALE
Ralph Crosses
DANBYDALE
Fat Betty
Botton Cross
Margary Stone
Rosedale Branch
North Eastern Railway
Esklets
FRYUP
Old coal Pits
Loose Howe
Pannier Trod
Botton Head
Blowath crossing
Blakey Inn
GLAISDALE
Cammon stone
Blakey Junction
Shunnor Howe
Rudland Rigg
Un Metalled Road
FARNDALE
BRANSDALE
Blakey Bank
Kilns
East Mines
Kilns
ROSEDALE
Depots
Blakey
Sled Shoe
West Mines
Bell End
River Seven
Sheriffs pit
Thorgill
Milburn Arms
Abbey
Rigg
Bank Top Chimney
Bank 1 in 3
Hartoft
Three Howes
Hollins Open cast mine
Ainhowe Cross
Road
Glass Holes
Spaunton Moor
Miles
0
1
2
3
4
5
Hutton-le-Hole
Askew
Ryedale Folk Museum
Lastingham
Spaunton

Contents

I
Foreword

The History of Rosedale is a part of and dovetails into the story of England, and the author has lived near it and with it all his life. He has researched it, dug it up, photographed it and, above all being a native of these moors and dales, he has the 'feeling' for it.

This book is the sum of many years work and is about Rosedale from its earliest times to the present. From Prehistory through the period of the Beaker Man – The Ancient Britons – The Roman Occupation – The Saxons, Danes and Normans down through the Great Ironstone Mining Era it is the continuing story of those people who have lived and died in Rosedale, sometimes a violent story but always an interesting one.

II
General Introduction

The Cleveland Hills are the backbone of the North York Moors National Park running from the Hambleton Hills in the west for about 40 miles to the rugged cliffs of the North Yorkshire Coast in the east.

From the central spine of hills, which rise to almost 1,450 feet, run watersheds in the form of dales to the north and south. These minor streams run into the River Esk in the north and the rivers Rye and Derwent to the south. The Esk flows through a beautiful valley some 20 miles to the North Sea at Whitby, while the Rye and Derwent run a longer course to the Ouse which in turn flows into the Humber and out to the sea at Hull.

Rosedale is on the south side of the hills and is a well wooded, somewhat narrow valley running north and south for about 8 miles. The main village is Rosedale Abbey, situated in the geographical centre of the National Park. It is the site of the old priory and is a small and very pretty village with a mild but bracing climate being sheltered by the surrounding hills. The scars of the 19th century mining have almost disappeared under bracken and heather.

The main areas of the dale include Thorgill, a small hamlet on the west side, sheltering under the cragg of the same name; Updale, on the east side, where many rows of miners' cottages have been turned into 'weekend cottages' while Hartoft at the south east end of the dale is really a very picturesque dale in its own right.

One feature of Rosedale is the number of derelict and ruined houses which date from the 19th century mining era when the dale became a little 'Klondyke'. In 1851 the population was 548 and by 1871 it had grown to 2,839, the heyday of the mining boom. By 1901 it had declined to 1,396 while in 1961 the figure was 286.

Every year many 'Dalesfolk' make their way back to the dale recalling the good years and the hard times of the late 20's and early 30's when the mines closed forever.

The Rosedale Show in the middle of August is an annual pilgrimage for many people.

Today the dale lives on amid the changing beauty of the seasons – the 'Greening' of the moors in spring, the wonderful variety of wild flowers and blossoms in early summer, the glowing purples of the heather in August and September, the deep red of the mountain ash berries in early autumn followed by the russet colours of dying bracken until winter covers all with a dazzling white cloak broken only by the dark greens of the forests.

Finally, what of the future? For the youngsters of the dale it is not very promising. Most of them were born and bred in the freedom of the dale, have great affection for it and would like to live and work here. Farming, the Forestry Commission, and more lately tourism, provide some work but not enough and all too soon they must leave the dale to find work – often not to return.

We are grateful to Mr. W. J. L. Young for allowing the History of Rosedale to be republished.

The staff at High Shop – Rosedale East. 1925. As late as 1930 the shop still had a staff of five.

III
Geological Background

The geological background of the dale is the Jurassic series of rock and shale underlying the major portion of the North East Yorkshire moors. It was formed by the gradual silting of the deltic beds, once the estuary of a great river. Atmospheric and water erosion, winter snows, frosts, spring thaws, rain and storm, rather than violent volcanic upheaval have formed the main factors in the formation of our beautiful dales, and the rolling moorland ridges that lie between them.

A noted geologist once said – 'In no part of England is the relation of surface topography to the nature of the underlying rocks, more instructively displayed than in our district'.

Like Roseberry Topping, which can be seen from Ralph Cross, the rounded hills of Rosedale – Abbey Head and Bell End – were formed by the erosion of softer beds of rock around a hard cap of gritstone or ironstone. Dr. Frank Elgee in his outstanding book on the Moorlands of North East Yorkshire (1912) describes a similar round hill in Fryup.

'In accounting for this hill we shall explain a similar one in Rosedale which affords a key to the problem. On its eastern side Rosedale has a large tributary gill debouching into it (Northdale), the lower parts of which are separated from the main valley by a high and narrow ridge of moorland capped with massive esturine sandstone. Beyond the end of the ridge is a deep gap penetrating to the Middle Lias (shale) and bounded on the south by a prominent hill of Upper Lias above Rosedale Abbey village, and precisely agreeing with the round hill in Fryup.'

A close inspection of the high narrow ridge reveals the fact that the summit sandstone at its termination is wider than the same rock half a mile further to the north, where it is less than 150 yards across. Now erosion, working upon this neck of rock, will wear away the narrow part long before the wider end of the ridge which will consequently form an outlier of oolite surrounded by lias.

Erosion still continuing, the neck, now composed of softer lias, will be worn into a pass or coll. In time the outlier loses its sandstone capping and a round hill of Upper Lias shale will have formed. It is easy to see that the hills of Rosedale and Fryup have been formed in a similar fashion.

The lias shales below beds of harder rock erode quickly and cause dipping of the strata, especially on the western slopes due to the rocks readily giving way along the lines of joint. These can be seen to advantage at Thorgill, where, west of Gill Bank, three great dips are formed, the upper capped by an impressive line of crags. Even more spectacular are those in Fryup Head forming a remarkable undercliff series of folds and rounded 'alps'.

The gritstone forms a line of exposed rock at Hob Crag on the road to Thorgill and at Cummerheaf, where it was extensively quarried. Crinoid Grit of the Scarborough Beds outcrops in Rosedale West and on Spaunton Moor. It was used for the manufacture of querns and millstones. The lower portion of the dale enters the corallian limestone at the foot of Cropton Bank, where it narrows into a gorge-like wooded valley. Here were many lime-kilns and quarries, now operated by larger companies at Pickering and Appleton Common. Much lime was led into the dale in exchange for moor-coal in the 17th–19th centuries.

Some of the 'rounded hills' in Rosedale are emphasised by trees.

IV
Prehistoric Times

The first evidence of human activity in the district comes from Star Carr in the eastern end of the Vale of Pickering – the remnants of a glacial lake some 32 miles long by 4 to 8 miles wide. These folk lived mainly by hunting and fishing; they had deer-antler worked harpoons or 'leisters' rather like eel-spears used in modern times; also mattocks or adzes of elk antler, as well as hundreds of flint tools and flakes. They were skilled carvers of wood and bone, making birch-bark containers and canoes which they paddled along the reedy shores of the lake to the brushwood landing stage where they lived. Amongst the animals they hunted were red and roe deer, elk, bear, wild ox, badger, boar, fox, pine-marten, beaver and hare. Several species of birds including crane and stork – no doubt shot with the bow and arrows were also found. The hunters were assisted by large wolf-like dogs and probably, like the Lapps, herded semi-domesticated animals for food and skins. These remains, the earliest of their kind in Britain, are dated by C14 and pollen analysis to 9,500 years ago.

These hunters could well have roamed into Rosedale, we have traces of similar folk from heaps of flint chippings found on the moors around the dale heads. These 'microliths' as they are called denote the working floors of tents or, turf and timber huts now long vanished; but from pollen evidence by experts such as Prof. G. W. Dimbleby, we can learn something of their environment. Instead of miles of treeless purple heather or bracken, there were dense forests of pine and birch, gradually giving place to oak, ash, alder, and even lime trees. As these forests were cleared by fire or by accidental or deliberate human activity, large clearings over-grown with hazel scrub appeared; later still these became the first cultivated plots or intakes. It is likely they herded the long-horned wild ox and reindeer with the aid of dogs and followed the animals in their seasonal migrations.

Sometime in the second or third century BC, the folk of the Neolithic, or

New Stone Age began to cultivate the clearings and to attack the forests with superior polished flint and stone axes. These tools are found to the present day, especially in Hartoft and on the limestone hills, and a few have turned up on the high moors around dale head. They were skilled wood workers, probably making timber huts and though no one has yet found a dwelling of these people their arrow-heads of leaf-shaped flints are plentiful, denoting hunting activity. The forest teemed with game, which kept the cooking pots full and the black-gritty pottery they used has been found at Spaunton, Thornton Dale and elsewhere in Ryedale. Trade and barter in stone axes of volcanic ash from the Lake District is proved by examples from Lowna, Hutton-le-Hole and Kirkbymoorside (in the Ryedale Folk Museum).

By the time of the so-called Bronze-Age (about 2,000 BC) people using a superior type of pottery called Beaker Ware had infiltrated into the district. Their remains are found under long and round barrows in the Pickering area, mainly from the Ryedale Windypits – deep fissures in the limestone where they disposed of their dead and their food refuse in the shape of piles of animal bones consisting of, red and roe deer, wild ox, pig, sheep, goats, snails and sea shells, and large and powerful dogs.

They were slender folk, suffering from deformities of the ankle joints from long periods of squatting, probably to avoid from sitting on the damp rocks of the fissures. Caves and fissures made ready-finished homes for people in this, and much later ages. Similar rock-shelters no doubt will be found in the crags of the dale sides. Innovations of the period were superior barbed and tanged flint arrow-heads, pierced stone axe-hammers and jet and bog-oak ornaments. There are several examples in the Scarborough and Ryedale Museums.

Beakers from the Pickering district are akin to those from Holland and the Low Countries.

Bronze was very rare, traded from the continent, but was later more plentiful and was manufactured in Ireland from native copper and Cornish tin; later a lead content was added.

The most impressive relics of the middle bronze age are the Tumuli or Barrows that form bumps or mounds on every moorland horizon. Called 'Howes' by the later Scandinavian settlers, they were prominent landmarks, usually by ancient trackways or ridge roads, marked later by pannier trods or hollow-ways. There are three such mounds close to Rosedale Chimney, about 70–100 ft. in diameter and 6–12 ft. high, all dug into by past seekers for pots or relics – such as the pot-hunting squires of Pickering in the mid 19th century. They are now protected by the Historic Buildings Commission which have the power to fine people who interfere with them. A large example close to the Lion Inn at Blakey was used as a cock-pit – the hollow left by the robbers was a convenient 'main' where enthusiasts could gather and see any suspicious stranger approaching. These burial mounds have rings of large stones set around their perimeters, and are constructed of stones, turf, or sandy soil – sometimes a combination of all three. Often they have a stone cist or box-like burial chamber in which were laid inhumations – long perished owing to the acid moorland soil – or cremations, which usually survive – sometimes with urns or food vessels and other offerings to the departed. In the Western Howes, east of Ralph Cross, small urns with cremated bones and a fine axe-hammer were found by Canon Atkinson who dug over 100 of these burial mounds. His collection lies in the cellars of the British Museum, never on view to the public – a sad state of affairs that should be remedied by its loan to the Dorman Museum, Middlesbrough, or any local collection with ready access to the public.

One of the most illuminating of the mounds of this period was Loose Howe at 1,419 ft. above the sea at Rosedale Head, close to the road to Ralph Cross and Fat Betty. It was opened in 1937 by members of the I.C.I. W.E.A. Class under the direction of Mrs. H. W. Elgee. The howe, about 70 ft. wide and 6 ft. high, was of turf capped by a covering of stones and surrounded by a ring of upright boulders. It covered the primary burial of an early bronze age man, interred in a tree trunk boat shaped coffin of oak 8 ft. long 2 ft. 3 ins. wide, with two similar canoe shaped dug-outs,one acting as lid and the other alongside the larger boat. The vessels had curved prows and a slot for a rudder. The remains of a skin cloak, leggings, and shoes, were found with the scanty remains of the man – also a small bronze dagger or knife. Hazel branches and nuts indicated a forest clearing as shown by the pollen samples of turf barrows on the Cleveland Hills (Dimbleby, G. W. Antiquity 1961). Higher up in the howe was a disturbed cremation burial with a broken urn, a fine stone axe-hammer, a broken bronze dagger, a bronze trefoil-headed pin, unique in that no other of its type has been found in a British barrow. Although a bone prototype was found at Brough on Humber, it was a central European product traded along with the knives and daggers. With it was a small cup, of the kind known as 'incense' cups, though of uncertain use. Evidence of early pilfering was shown by the finding of sherds of Norman pottery in the hole dug 4 ft. into the centre of the howe.

Not far away are Fryup peat holes where the worked horn of bos (ox) primigenius was dug out at the base of the peat, with a jet beaker-type button in the block of peat. The analysis of the peat showed there was open country, woodland glades, much hazel scrub, with heather appearing in the open clearings and not much grass. Oak, pine and alder flourished, the timber for the boats was at hand, but where were they used or were they just symbolical, like the boat of the dead in Egyptian ritual?

Groups of smaller cairns of stone can be seen on Spaunton Moor and south of Abraham's Hut, a forty-foot cairn opposite Hartoft End. Several were destroyed by the forestry on the Hancow ridge, one contained a tanged and barbed arrow-head, but no trace of cremation or inhumation has been found in many examined in recent years. On Danby Rigg they are associated with ringworks and ruined walling, possibly of ancient fields, also cross ridge earthworks, which can be seen on Castleton Rigg, High Stone Dyke, and on the road to Egton Bridge at William Howe, just above the moor gate on the Egton side. No relics of the late Bronze-Age have yet come from the dale, but the small cairns mentioned above may overlap into this period. There are traces of round or oval huts by the river in the lower end of the dale that may prove to have been inhabited at this time.

Bronze Age burial mounds or tumuli are a common feature on the North York Moors. Many were robbed of their grave goods during Victorian times but all are now protected monuments.

V

The Iron Age

This period began about 600 BC, merging with the late bronze age. Though evidence from Rosedale is scanty it must have been of importance as at the end of this period of some 600–700 years Rosedale iron was sought out and worked. Carts or chariots were in use on the limestone hills above Pickering, iron fittings coated with bronze, horse bits, nave hubs, etc., have come from burials of this period at Cawthorn and Pexton Moor. On Levisham Moor the complete outline of post-holes and ditches of an iron-worker's hut was found and in the centre of this, a complete smelting furnace or 'bloomery' was intact, this is 1,000 years earlier than any others found in the district. A report, 'Levisham Moor. Archaeological Investigations 1957–1978', has been published jointly by the North York Moors National Park Committee and the Scarborough Archaeological and Historical Society, 1983.

VI
The Roman Era

Worked iron-slag and iron tools are plentiful on all sites found in Ryedale in this period. A large timber-framed aisled farmhouse was discovered under two parallel grassy mounds at Spaunton, yielding pottery and hand-mills of 3rd and 4th century AD; nearby was a smaller hut and a sophisticated villa has been excavated near Beadlam–Helmsley. (By Dr. I. M. Stead for the D.O.E. 1969). At Cawthorn, east of Cropton are four Roman practise camps excavated by Dr. J. L. Kirk and Prof. Ian Richmond in the 1920s, they showed 1st and early 2nd century occupation for training troops possibly of the ill-fated ninth legion which disappears from history soon afterwards. From these camps a paved military road was laid towards the coast north of Whitby. This is called Wade's Causeway from a legendary giant of fame in the Mulgrave area where he is supposed to be buried and of his wife 'Bell', who carried the stones in her apron 'broadcasting them behind her like sowing corn,' said a local man. This road, lost after the military events of the second century, was rediscovered by local historians and a Goathland keeper, James Patterson who traced it over Wheeldale moors to that village, where the M.O.W. excavated it in 1919–20. The massive paving stones and upright kerbs holding the raft of stone on its cambered ridge, can still be seen and visited by walking from Stape or by car from Goathland. It is described fully in the Scarborough and District Archaeological Society Report No 4.

Possibly the greatest benefit the Romans brought to the Rosedale district was improved methods of farming, heavier ploughs, rotary hand-mills or querns, which are found in the dales of Danby and Hartoft, and especially on the limestone hills already producing good wheat and barley. In the dales and moors the natives carried on much as in the previous bronze and iron ages, using the 'ard' or one-way plough or a version of a digging stick like a turf-spade. Querns for grinding the corn were made from the local freestone from the outcrop near Ainhowe Cross. Loomweights testify weaving, and small sheep bones are common in the refuse of their huts. Malton was a garrisoned fort and York the H.Q. of the northern command, both within a day's ride of Rosedale, so trade and better and better pottery, including imported Samian ware, was obtainable for those who could afford them. (Relics from the local sites in the Ryedale Folk Museum).

That the locals had coins is certain from the finds on the sites, and from the discovery of a hoard of 3rd century date in a peat bog North West of Hamer House. Some were barbarous imitations of current issues. Remains of Roman occupation including pottery, bones and flue-tiles have been found in Newtondale 3 miles north of Pickering and the same distance from Rosedale.

The Ryedale Folk Museum displays a range of Roman pottery discovered locally.

Wade's Causeway is one of the best preserved sections of Roman road in the country. Built about A.D. 80 it linked the Roman Fort at Malton with camps at Cawthorn near Pickering and Lease Rigg above Grosmont.

VII
Saxon-Viking Settlement

The Saxon settlement was very gradual, lasting over 200 years and probably made little difference to the lives of those dwelling on the moor edges of the dale, or in the gaps made in the forested valley. They had little to lose and changed one master for another with ease. Hints of them still linger in place names, Cummerheaf crag, 'Home of the Cymery' (or Welshmen) as the Saxons called the native celtic population. Glaisdale from Celtic, 'Grey, Wardle Rigg and Wapley, 'Welshmen's Rigg and Welshmen's Pool', also the numerous 'Pen' hill or 'howe' names. Apart from two coins of the 7th and 9th centuries and pottery from the eastern end of the Vale of Pickering, we have little evidence of Saxons, apart from the carved stones in the churches such as Lastingham and Middleton, and the details in Bede's History of the English Church and People written in the 8th century. The Norse and Danish raiders and later settlers did make their influence felt in the dales towards the 10th–11th centuries. They left a wealth of place-names in Rosedale, 'Rossi' is said to be a personal name, but Ekwall points out Rossi was an old Norse name for a horse. Thorgill comes from Thor the god of thunder, thwaite, a clearing and later a meadow is common; gill, sike, slack and breck are all names from this period. A sherd of pottery of 9th century date has been found in Danby; Kildale church had several Viking burials, in fact this dale has produced archaeological evidence of all periods from the old stone age, in contradiction of a recent writer on medieval monastic settlement who states that the dales were not settled until the 13th century.

The best representation of a Viking warrior can be seen on a grave-cross in Middleton by Pickering church which was part of the honour of Rosedale and also its parish church for a considerable time. Bound dragons of Norse-celtic tradition are carved on other crosses, one of which shows a hunter with a clumsy horse-like stag and two hounds. They were fond of gay clothes, gold and silver ornaments, and had expensive curtains or hangings to keep the draught out of their halls. From the saga's we gather they were skilled iron workers – 'Egil Ska llagrimson was a notable iron-smith and had a great smelting of ore in winter time'. No doubt the smoke of iron furnaces rose into the air from the dales at this time.

Like the celtic folk before them they lived in separate farmsteads rarely in nucleated villages. The houses were usually of wood and turf, though stone was used where it was plentiful. They were of the 'long-house' type, long and narrow, dark and smokey, with the humans in one end and animals in the other, divided only by a cross-passage, or a wattle partition. The roofs were of thatch-heather, rye-straw, or turf. They were the forerunners of the cruck-framed long house so prevalent in the dales for many centuries. An 18th century reconstruction of one can be seen at the Ryedale Folk Museum, giving a splendid glimpse of how people lived in those days, all under one roof, family, stock and poultry.

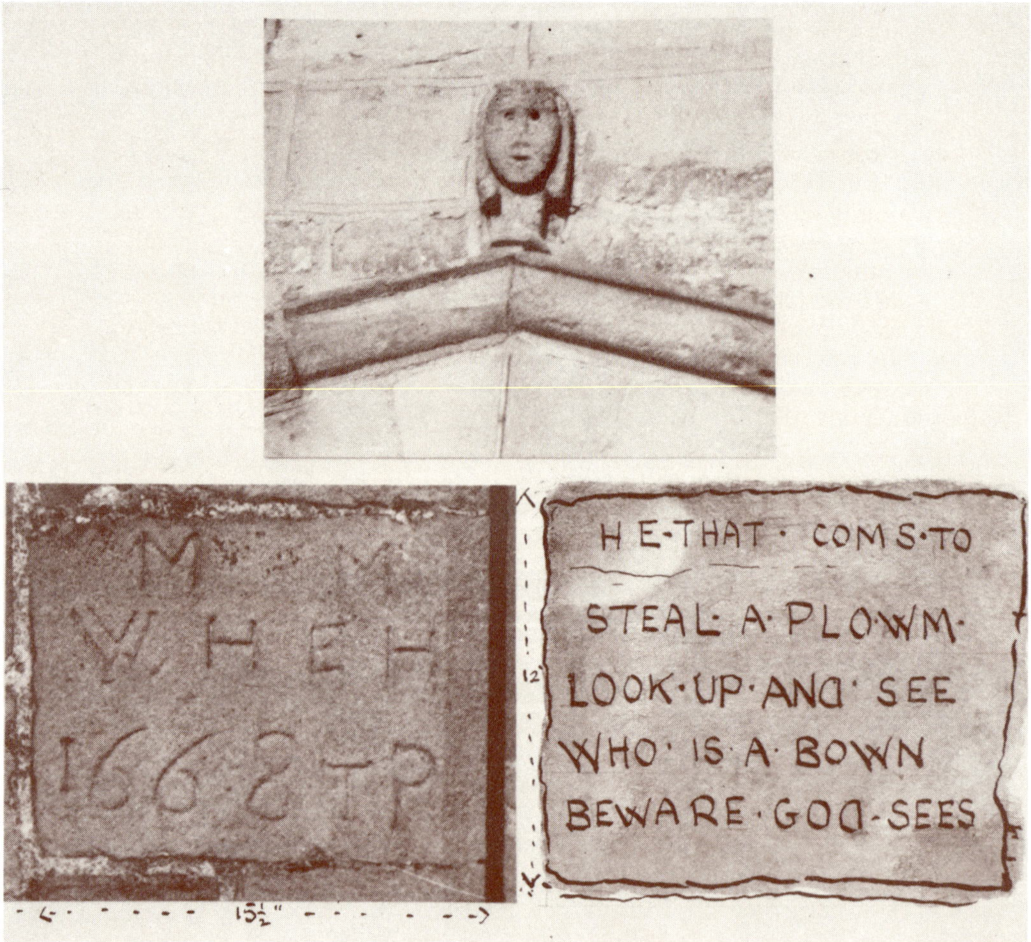

Carvings and inscriptions over the doorway to Beck House, Cropton.

VIII
Norman-Medieval Period

The Norman Conquest changes things more rapidly. The battles of Stamford Bridge, the rising of Earl Morcar against William the Conqueror at York must have taken its toll of lives. Earl Morcar held Middleton, part of the Soke of Pickering, before the conquest. Later it went to the King and was part of the Royal Forest of Pickering. Rosedale is not mentioned in the great Domesday record, though it probably was recorded as part of Middleton and Pickering, which was worth £88 in the days of Edward the Confessor, but only 20/4d by 1068 AD. This was thought to be the result of the Normans' scorched earth policy of vengeance but the possibility of Scottish raids cannot be ruled out.

Then came a period of rebuilding old monasteries or the founding of new ones. The King gave land in Lastingham, Spaunton, Hutton, Baschebi,* a 'lost vill' probably Askew where there were four farms in the 19th century. He also gave the monk Stephen of Whitby, the west side of Rosedale to the river Seven, which apparently was part of Spaunton Manor and may have been held by Gamel, the Saxon, before the conquest. Stephen was also rebuilding the Saxon Monastic foundation of Lastingham which was said to be in ruins and was probably neglected due to the troubles mentioned above or even, as some think, as a result of Viking raids. Later the King claimed hunting rights as Rosedale and Spaunton Moor were part of the west ward of the Pickering royal forest.

A family called de Rosedale were probably granted tenancy of crown lands in Rosedale East, and possibly Cropton and Middleton, Liddle in Cumberland was given to Turgissius Brundos in 1120; and in 1130, William Brundros and his wife Godeheuld paid 2 marks of silver to the crown for his

*The site of Baschebi probably lies south of Askew, near Hamley Hagg or towards Appleton High Cross. Finds from this area are described by Mrs. M. R. Allison in 'Transactions of the Scarborough Archaeological Society' 1980.

estates in Yorkshire. This was probably the William de Rosedale, who gave Kershope in Cumberland to St. Peter's Hospital York in 1135; he gave other property to Jedburgh Priory. There is a charter, confirmed by King John, witnessed at Scarborough on Feb. 3rd 1201, which confirms Rosedale Priory, a gift which William de Rosedale had made, and which his son, another Turgis, had confirmed. William de Rosedale must be considered the founder of the Priory and not Robt. de Stuteville as is stated in popular accounts of Rosedale. The young Turgis was at Newcastle with Henry II in 1158, where he witnessed a document of the King of Scotland as Turgissius de Rossendala. A Guy de Rosedale is mentioned about 1170, and a Robt. de Russedal witnessed a charter of Robert de Stuteville III, about 1183, the date when the major local estates seem to have been transferred to the Stuteville family.

The Stutevilles were a Norman family who came over soon after the conquest from their Normandy estate; Robt. de Stuteville I was given the lands of Hugh Fitzbaldric, the Sheriff of York, but lost them through being on the wrong side in early baronial wars. His lands were given to Nigel d'Aubigny (later Mowbray) by King Henry I but Robt. III his grandson, was able to get 10 knights' fees back from Mowbray including the manor of Kirkbymoorside (1166). Other members of the Stuteville family gave grants to Rosedale Priory. The last of the Stutevilles, Joan, married Hugh Wake before 1229 and in 1281–2 Baldwin Wakes's 'Honour of Rosedale' included the knight's fee of Middleton, with Cropton, Cawthorn, Wrelton and Aislaby, sub-let to others for parts of knight's fees (service to the overlord and the king in time of war). This fee also included lands held by the Knights Templars and Old Malton Priory.

So Rosedale was divided into three portions in the Middle Ages, the Priory held lands under the Stutevilles and Wakes, the west side already was under the Abbot of St. Mary's, York, supervised by his underlord at Spaunton Manor, John de Spaunton (or Spanton, the family name) and the head of the dale called Swineheved, a mistake for Sevenhead which was held by the canons of Guisborough Priory under de Brus of Skelton Castle. In a charter of 1223, Peter de Brus gave the canons all the wood on either side of the Seven, also leave to build sheepfolds, cultivate and enclose, and to work iron. The boundary was Blakehou (Cockpit Howe at Blakey), following the road to Crucem Rudulpi (Ralph Cross its first mention), also the wood of Bothine (Botton Cross), Friho Troch, (now Fryup Trough), a name of interest akin to Trossachs, possibly meaning 'Spikey', a reference to the remarkable spikes and crags of its tumbled undercliff. This charter emphasises the extent of woodland on what is now treeless dalehead or moorland. All the tenants of the district were subject to forest laws, Rosedale is described as 'a nest of poachers', inhabitants of the dale and Hartoft were frequently hauled up before the courts of Pickering, the 'Eyre' of the forest, for offences of this nature also for taking 'green' wood or 'assarting' (enclosing); even the Prioress was summoned for this. They were allowed timber for building and making carts, waggons or tools, and dead wood for burning and we have long lists of allocations by the foresters of 'forks' or 'siles' for cruck-framed houses. The de Rosedales may have built the motte and bailey castle on top of Cropton Bank, where they had a splendid prospect of their domains. The motte is a circular mound of earth 150 ft. wide and 25 ft. high; it housed a wooden tower or keep, built on wooden 'stilts'. The bailey or outwork, a bank with palisade, surrounded by a deep ditch, held the domestic quarters, stables, cowsheds, and wells or fishponds. This type of early Norman castle can be seen depicted on the Bayeaux Tapestry. Some like Pickering, grew in strength by adding stone defences at a later date. It is not certain whether Cropton had stone works, though in the 15th century there was a half-timbered or stone hall of the Horsley family, built partly over the ditch of the motte. In the reign of Edward III at the inquest on Thomas Wake it is stated that Cropton Castle was in ruins (1349). That was the year of the Black Death, the pestilence that wiped out half the population of the North and we are told Cropton decreased in value owing to this. A small Norman chapel stood until the 19th century when it was pulled down to make way for the present church of St. Gregory.

Beck House, a substantial farmstead in the vale below the castle was said to have been built from stones of the Hall Garth of Cropton. It was certainly an early foundation for long before this it was held by the Bygot or Bigod family, Hugh Bygot was a speculator in wool in the mid 13th century. In the 14th century intakes and dykes were raised on what is now moorland west of Askew on Tranmire Plain. They may have been in connection with sheep farming.

IX
The Priory

Rosedale Abbey as it is usually called, was actually a small priory of the Cistercian Order, dedicated to St. Mary and St. Lawrence although some sources say it was Benedictine, it was more likely the foundation of William de Rosedale. It consisted of 9 nuns supervised by a prioress, and a few lay workers, mainly farmers or shepherds. Sometimes it had 12 sacks of wool for sale annually, a good average for a small establishment. They were given sheep strays at Middleton, Newton, Cawthorn and at Lockton, where Alan Malcake gave them an oxgang (15–18 acres) a toft and croft (house and field), the site of a sheep-fold, an acre of land in Ketilcroft, Abunscar (Ketil's plot of land above the scar) possibly above Dalby; also timber from the forest of Staindale (not the miserable larch forest of the present day but the noble oak wood that grew there in the Middle Ages). There was also pasture for 200 sheep at Lockton where a lane now called Hostess Lane was said to be where the nuns pastured their sheep, but this place name, sometimes given as Austers, could have derived from the old Saxon Eowestre, a sheepfold.

William de Bolebeck gave them 2 oxgangs, a toft and croft, and pasture for 300 sheep, possibly at Newton or Levisham. (Over 2,000 sheep in 1308). So they had large flocks here and on the moors of Rosedale East which Robert de Stuteville gave them in the 12th century, soon after the foundation. Rosedale East stretched from Peter de Brus's boundaries (Millfield Bridge?) southwards to Anchow (Hankow), now a ruin on the road down Hartoft Rigg, to the river Seven following Smalesikes (now Swalesike), still the boundary of Hartoft down by Mill Farm. He also gave them the meadow of Baggethwaite (baggi's clearing-meadow), to (Amoth) an old Norse name meaning the junction of two streams; in this case the confluence of Northdale Beck and the Seven, close to the priory. There was an iron forge in Baggethwaite, the smoke and the noise of which annoyed the nuns so it

Rosedale Priory ruins before 1850. The belfry on the left is all that remains today. The Priory was established by the Cistercian Order and had nine nuns and a prioress.

Chapel Choir c.1910/12.

must have been close to the priory. The clue to this came when Arthur Champion recalled that his uncle Page had told of a mass of iron slag and charcoal being found when the foundations of the Lecture Hall were dug in 1873. This could have been the remains of the forge that annoyed the nuns as Eustace de Stuteville eventually removed it from the original site. In the 14th century the priory had several visitations by Archbishop Greenfield. Most of these concerned chastisements, penances, or financial troubles. The nuns were forbidden to wear mantles or garments of gay colours; the prioress and sub-prioress were told not to allow puppies to enter the church and impede the devotions. Evidently Chaucer's verse about the prioress on the pilgrimage with her gay apparel and 'small hounds', was not far off the mark! Nuns were sent to other houses (Handale near Loftus), as a penance.

On November 21st 1322, the Scots after the battle of Byland when they chased King Edward II to the gates of York, raided Rosedale damaging the priory so severely that the nuns had to be sent to other houses until repairs were carried out. Only five nuns are named, but others can be accounted for in various nunneries. They were only readmitted to Rosedale in June 1323. In the lay subsidy list of the 14th century, eight nuns are named. There was trouble with a nun, Joan Fletcher; eventually she left to become the head of Baysdale nunnery. At the Suppression there were eight nuns and the prioress, who received a state pension; they employed 12 men and boys. No doubt there were grumbles in the dale at the loss of employment. Possibly there was a priory school for local children, for in spite of their lapses they gave moral and secular education, and services in the church on Sundays and Holy days.

The action of Henry VIII and his minister, Thomas Cromwell of suppressing the monastaries in 1535, was bitterly resented, so much so that the destruction of the 'abbey' as it was called, was later attributed to Oliver Cromwell, even though he was active 100 years later!

At the end there were two small bells in the campanile or belfry, valued at 10/-, gilt plate, chalice, and a goblet, annual value at the close of about £37.

The average size of the priory church was estimated by the late R. W. Crosland to be 60–76 ft. in length by 18–20 ft. wide, probably a simple nave and chancel, without a transept. The V.C.H. says it had the remains of the North West angle of the transept, but most of the priory churches of this type in Yorkshire, have no transepts, so it is unlikely Rosedale was an exception to this rule. The priory buildings survived until 1849 and the cloister had been converted into dwelling houses. The restored chancel was in use as the parish church and the conventual buildings formed the old manor house of the East side described in 1649 as 'large and having several rooms, much decayed, roofed with thatch' – now the Milburn Arms.

The Rev. G. Young in his History of Whitby, Vol. 1 1817; confirms the state of the cloister converted into houses and barns. He writes: 'In this square, on the E side are some tombstones of nuns with crosses carved upon them. The name "Catherine Meger", is legible, a slab with the name "Marie" exists.' Dugdale in 'Monasticon' Vol.14 p.319 gives details of the 1328 confirmation of gifts to Rosedale Priory – Alan, son of Ulf – one messuage in Middleton and 4½ roods of land next to the stone cross in the same village!

There is a nice sketch of about 1780, showing the picturesque ruins, all swept away by the surge of Victorian modernization that took place when the mining era began and which lasted, as we shall see, about 70 years. The priory had stood almost 700, and still in 1850 was one of the most complete relics of a small priory in the North of England. All we have left now is one small turret or belfry and in it a vice or stair. There are also traces of a large west window and opposite, in a garden, on top of a shed is a weathered sundial and nearby are the foundations of a second turret. On the north door of the present church which is built of the colourful priory sandstone, is a lintel from the cloister inscribed Omnia Vanitas – 'All is vanity'. The large window in the wall of the vestry is late 14th century, and two trefoil heads stand at the west end of the present church, possibly from the cloisters. There are similar balusters and a head over the reroofed St. Cedd's well at Lastingham, brought from Rosedale in the mining era. The bones of a tall man were found at the east end of the church, in a broken stone coffin, one end of which was made into a seat which stood by the church for many years.

So ended the house of worship founded by noble families for the refuge and education of their daughters in an age of strife and uneasy living. After the rebuilding of the church in 1840 a major restoration was carried out in 1893; William Milburn and Albert de Land Long contributed £200 towards the cost. The roof was taken off and the ceiling replastered, and the windows reglazed. A carved oak lectern was given by George Leeman of York, who had interests in the mines and railway. The registers date from 1610. The tomb of Thomas Peirson, founder of a charity to educate three children in Rosedale and two in Hartoft, stands on the south side of the path, but the inscription is illegible. He died at Heygate in 1720. The church is still in regular use for worship and the vicar resides in the dale. A new vicarage was built in 1901–2, but is now a private house and the vicar has gone to live much nearer the church below East Lodge.

On the dissolution of the priory, on July 9th 1538 – together with Keldholme priory – it was granted to Ralph Neville, Earl of Westmorland, who leased it to William Smithdike of the household of the King at £7.9s.0d. per annum for 21 years. On the de-possession of the Earl, owing to his part in the Pilgrimage of Grace, they were forfeit to the Crown; James I granted them to George Villiers, Duke of Buckingham, who sold them to Charles Duncombe.

When the Manor of Rosedale was leased in 1576 to Ambrose, Earl of Warwick K.G. and Ann, his wife, there were 40 farms and 6 mills. The Nun's mill is mentioned in 1330, it was a water-mill, doubtless on the site of the present mill buildings near the village. It had two leats, one from the Seven at Waterhouse Well (called the Monk's well, probably a mistake for nun's well); the other from Northdale beck; perhaps there were two mills in the past? The mill is shown on the old sketch of about 1840 as a thatched building with a wooden wheel; in the Black Gate Museum, Newcastle in 1938, there was part of a wooden hub with a spoke, labelled 'part of the Rosedale Abbey mill, donated by William Milburn'. The present mill rebuilding was by George Wilson, and is dated 1853.

Millfield Bridge, Updale must have been the site of a second watermill but no trace remains. In Thorgill the ruins of the old corn mill called 'Township Mill 1820', still stand by the little beck below the hamlet, it was already a ruin by 1860.

On the Seven below Mill Farm, east of the village, traces of a leat and a mound on the north bank of the river, mark the site of Walker mill, a fulling mill. William Hill was the last fuller to work there. It was a process in which cloth was cleaned of grease and thickened. The fifth mill may have served Hartoft where there is a large dam opposite Spiers Bank Farm. Alternatively this could have been used for iron or coal mining wheels, as there was much activity in these occupations at Hartoft End between 1570–1590.

The sixth may have been higher up in Hartoft, or even Cropton Mill two miles lower downstream.

Group outside St. Lawrence School.

X
Rosedale Glass Workers

In the late 16th century during the great days of Queen Elizabeth's reign, French glass-workers, probably from the Weald of Kent where the noted Jean Carre set up a glass-house in 1567, began operations in Rosedale West.

The site was chosen for its supply of oak timber, siliceous sand, bracken (for potash and lime), and a plentiful amount of clay. Local freestone was used to erect a large furnace with two crucible holders, mainly for the production of vessel-glass. When the ingredients mentioned were mixed with 'cullet' (waste broken glass) a mixture or 'frit' was made and roasted for 48 hours to obtain a good 'metal' as the glass was called. The finished product was of excellent quality, consisting of goblets, flasks, tumblers, bottles and linen-smoothers, all in green 'forest glass'.

The furnace was 25 ft. long by 18 ft. wide with four wings, for annealing and pot-arching (finishing off pots or crucibles). When excavated it still stood 3 ft. 6 ins. high though badly eroded by weathering and bracken roots. There were three or four subsidiary ovens or hearths and the glass workers lived in the ruin now called Allen House with its two small intakes opposite Scugdale and Hartoft End.

The excavation was carried out by a joint effort of D. W. Crossley and F. A. Aberg, University lecturers and their students, also helpers from Ryedale Folk Museum who later removed the stones dismantled during the excavations to re-erect them in the grounds of the Folk Museum.

They were assisted by a grant from Pilkington Brothers, the Glass Makers, and Arthur Pilkington opened the restored furnace in its medieval-type timbered shed, in May 1970 at Hutton-le-Hole.

Research by Mr. J. Hurst of Hutton-le-Hole in the Lastingham Parish Registers showed that between 1570 and 1600 there was an influx of foreigners into the Parish. Several stange-sounding French and Huguenot family names appear and die out just as suddenly. One actually records the death of the wife of Amabie the Glassman in 1593. This fits in with the conclusions of the archaeologists that the furnace was of French type and its life was short as by 1615 an edict forbade the use of oak timber for glass and iron working because it was becoming scarce for ship and house-building.

These strangers in this islolated part of the dale with their possibly illegal furnace had little contact with the local folk apart from the foresters and quarrymen, hence all knowledge and records of them appear to have been lost. Only a vague tradition of 'Glass Holes' remained, though one man knew where they were sited – he was John Dale of Hollins, who showed the writer the site in 1948.*

At that time he produced a piece of glassy slag which closely resembled iron-slag, so that we thought it was the product of medieval bloomeries. It was not until 1968 that a trial dig showed that old John was right. There were two other local men who suspected that glassworking took place in or near the small quarry pits they called glass-holes on the ridge opposite the Blacksmiths Arms, Hartoft End. They were John Pennock who was brought up there, and whose father worked in a stone quarry close by, and John Bowes of Cropton, the Darley Estate mason. But it is due to John Dale we are able to uncover these remarkable furnaces.

*Glass Holes. A series of shallow quarry pits on the moor west of the site of the glass furnace. No glass or burnt debris found here but excavations of one in 1982 proved that under a layer of soft sandstone a deposit of siliceous sand could have been used for glass making. Report in Ryedale Historian no.12. 1984.

The re-constructed glass furnace in the Ryedale Folk Museum at Hutton-le-Hole.

XI
Moorland Crosses

Some of the ancient moorland crosses belong to the monastic period. Ralph Cross was already old in the 13th century, though writers in certain magazines insist it was erected to mark the spot where a man called Ralph from Danby lost his life in a blizzard. Actually there are two Ralph Crosses; Young Ralph, the more recent, by the main road, and Old Ralph standing on the highest point a quarter of a mile to the west at 1,420 ft. above the sea, which is visible from this point. Young Ralph replaced a wooden cross in the 17th century. They are associated with another about a mile eastwards, Fat Betty, a wheel-head on a massive stout base, hence the name; also with a standing stone far more ancient called Margary Bradley, or Margary Moorpout. Legend connects these three with meetings to settle boundary disputes between the prioresses of Rosedale and Baysdale, led by 'Ord Ralph Rosdil' their guide. They were lost in a roke or fog – very frequent at this point – and Ord Ralph found Sister Margary beside the ancient stone, and then went back for Sister Betty waiting by the cross named above; he led them to the cross roads where they held their meeting, now the site of Old Ralph's Cross. This tale is charmingly told by the late Wilfrid Crosland in his booklet 'Yorkshire Treasure' (1948). The custom of placing money or food on top of Ralph Cross is also said to originate from monastic times, although it was carried out long before, like the custom of placing food or cream in a hollow cup stone for the hob or fairy. This was usual in Roman Times as an offering to the 'Genii Loci' the local spirit. Cropton Cross is connected with a similar practise:

'On Cropton Cross there is a cup
In that cup there is a sup,
Take that cup and drink that sup –
And put the cup back on the cross top.'

This sounds like an echo of the practise of the Saxon King Edwin, who

A feature of the North York Moors, many moorland crosses were erected as guide posts during mediaeval days. Ralph Cross is a prominent landmark and has been adopted as the National Park emblem.

Duck Bridge is a fine example of a medieval pack horse bridge over the River Esk. c. 1396.

ordered that a bronze cup be chained onto a stake or stone by every spring on the main highways (early 7th century AD.).

Fat Betty actually stands on the now disused pannier-trod to Danby. Botton Cross (from Botn – old Norse for a deep hollow), is by the old tracks to Danby and Fryup; Ainhowe or Ana Cross is 19th century, its older counterpart is in the crypt at Lastingham church.

Redman Cross nearer Rosedale, commemorates an old dale family of that name, but only its base-stone remains.

Other crosses have vanished, such as High Cross near Lastingham, though two survive on the road to Appleton-le-Moors, High and Low Crosses. It was only in 1719 that a by-law was passed ordering guide-stones or way markers to be set up on all used ways and high roads in the North Riding. Monastic trade brought roads into use that had been neglected since Roman times, Rievaulx charters mention several 'Magna vias' (Great roads), though few seem to have been paved. Blakey ridge road and Hartoft ridge (Hancow) road, also figure in 13th–14th century charters. Attributed to the monks, or the Quakers, are several paved pannier-trods, though substanial evidence is lacking. The pannier-trods were single flag causeways, flatstones set side by side, usually over boggy places, although one, George Gap Causeway, was formerly continuous from Rosedale Head (east) to Fryup Head, continuing in this dale by Long causeway and 'Street' houses to ancient settlements near Lealholme, where it branched near a stone inscribed Staithes, Whitby, Kirkbymoorside and Guisborough.

One of these led to Duck Bridge, a medieval bow-bridge, near Danby Castle, and others can be seen in Arncliffe woods and in lower Eskdale. In Rosedale some survive, they may be as late as 18th–19th century; one runs from the village by the old police house to White Bridge. It then went to Thorgill, where it survives west of Medd's farm. Eventually it lead to Moorlands Farm below Blakey ridge, where it joined another coming up from Millfield Bridge. At Moorlands, it passed right through the old farmstead, where the door had to be kept unlocked all the time. This must have been a nuisance to the occupants so not surprisingly the farm house, rebuilt in 1748, was eventually turned into a cow-house and a new dwelling built; the remains of the trod ran through the garden.

There is a legend of an old woman laying the stones similar to that told of Wade's causeway. The Trod to Millfield Bridge was called 'Battling Bridge

Hill' in 1549, and Battling Hills Lane later: but on whom and when they fought, legend is silent, probably a memory of Scots' raids in the 14th century.*

At Blakey we have 'pannierman's' spring and sieves (rushes). The old Inn was a meeting place for hucksters and dealers, and sheep sales took place there, this has been revived recently. Horses were changed here after the long pull up from Castleton and the steeper one from Rosedale. Pack horses were called 'gals' from Galloway ponies, they carried 'wackas' or panniers on each side, the lead horse had bells on its bridle to keep the rest, some 20–40 or more horses following. Much moor coal was taken to the lime-works at Hutton-le-Hole or Cropton by this transport as late as 1870–80 and droves of these animals (also donkeys), could be seen on the abbey green at Rosedale.

Eventually the main roads were widened and surfaced with limestone, whinstone, or local yellow sandstone. They were deeply rutted, muddy in winter and dusty in summer and on the hills such as the chimney bank massive offsets to divert rainwater into side gutters, gave the riders a nasty jolt. It was usual to put a metal shoe under the cart wheel to act as a brake, whilst descending: sometimes a horse was fastened behind to hold back the cart with a heavy load. Oxen were considered steadier on hills than horses and were used for draught until the late 19th century. It was in the 1930's that the great change to tarmac came to the roads, even much later for the moorland roads to Eskdale. The Bank was used for motor-club hill climbs in the 1920's, the late A. W. Champion, now at Castleton won three of these on an old motor bike he tuned-up himself in his Rosedale workshop.

*In the Humbestone Survey 1569 it states 'Thos Ward holds a cottage and close called Battel Bridge Hill.'

XII
Dalefolk

We have a few names recorded from the Middle Ages in the Coucher Book. Peter, son of Henry Young of Rosedale, on Wed. 30th of Jan. 1325, took and slew a hind in Sutherland with bow and arrows. Fined 13/4d. John, son of Abbas of Rosedale, on 22nd of July, wounded a hart in the forest of the abbot of Whitby, then followed it with bow and arrow, into the forest of Pickering, but did not take it; afterwards the Bailiff of the forest found it and took it to Pickering Castle. Shortly after Michaelmas, the same year, John slew a hart in Alantofts, Goathland; he took it home, then in the same place he wounded a hart, and was poaching again on Oct. 4th, but nemesis overtook him and he was outlawed!

Richard Moryn of Rosedale, on behalf of the Abbot of St. Mary's, York (evidently he was on the west side under Spaunton Manor) with others from Farndale; Ralph Head, Roger Milne, Walter and Robert Blackhouse (Blakey), along with a Spaunton man, killed two deer in the forest. All were outlawed. We do not know the fate of these unfortunates who were unlucky enough to be outlawed, though some certainly remained in the district as they were caught again at their old game. Perhaps they held out in the wilder parts of the dales, like their contemporaries in the Icelandic sagas, otherwise every man's hand was against them, and they could not have lasted long. Maybe they had a pact with the locals not to molest them in return for a share in the spoils of the chase. Many others were fined for letting cattle stray in the forest during the prohibited period (fence month), we have the case of John Monmouth, the forester, taking 2/- from William Miller of Rosedale, for permitting his six oxen to enter the forest. In the 14th century we have people who were fined for offences of Vert (destruction of timber), Abraham and John Knott (Knott is still the name of the hill on the road to Ralph's Cross), John son of Ralph of Beckhouse, William Tunge of Hartoft; Emma of Rosedale and Alice Head (Head House, Hartoft) are

The Old Turf Fire, Rosedale

Old Simpson and his wife (before 1900). Notice the turf-pan on the fire and the reckon crooks on the crane.

Rosedale Abbey Temperance Band. J. Champion (front right) was a notable conductor who made the Farndale Silver Band famous in the period 1910–1940.

named amongst the few females in the list. Taking into cultivation plots of land from the common (assarting) was another offence though some got away with it as the lord could take a yearly fine as rent and thus got improved land into the bargain. John Cook, Hugh Lamb, John Fox, William Hare, John Stirkherd all of Hartoft, appeared on this charge. Their names sound like a child's animal story, but they were so named after their occupation (or associations).

Very few families can trace their descent back to the Middle Ages, some go back about 200 years, Dowsons and Fletchers, though the Peirsons, Dryings and Redmans, and possibly Stricklands, are found in records of over 400 years ago.

The Parliamentary Surveys of monastic Crown lands in Rosedale are in the Public Record Office and give a very useful insight on the state of that part of Rosedale East.

These documents were compiled just after the Civil Wars in 1649, when crown lands were sold or leased by parliament. T. S. Willan commenting on them in the Yorks. Archaeological Journal for 1933 says: 'It is a striking commentary on the policy of the crown with regard to its possessions that the only relics of monastic property in their hands at this time were certain farms in Rosedale, the demesne lands of the Priory'.

The lease of Haygate* (now Heygate), occupied by Margaret Peirson, and that of Suggett's farm in Northdale, were only pieces of illegible rotting parchment, 'Rotten and consumed by lying in the ground during the late wars' said the surveyors as was also that of John Redman. The tenants had to bring their neighbours as witnesses to vouch for their claim on the tenancy.

This survey throws much light on the smallholders of the east side of the dale, it also shows that the monastic holdings were already enclosed, possibly as early as the 14th century; we also know stone walls were built at this time from medieval records of other dales. Secondly the farms were set in their own groups of fields, a contrast to Pickering where the open-field and strip cultivation of the Middle Ages was still in operation until the late 18th century. Traces of the old open-field husbandry existed in Rosedale, the names Northfield, South, East and Middle field recur through the surveys. Fields near the Priory show strips of rigg and furrow denoting the

*In the Humbestone Survey 1569 Haygate is called HAGGART and held by Thomas Willyamson also with Hangingstone Intake and certain closes.

Crowd listening to Rosedale Band playing on the village green. c.1900.

former existence of the medieval town field system. These tiny enclosed fields would take up much time in walling and access. On Thomas Peirson's farm of 169 acres, the largest in the Dale was divided into no fewer than 66 closes.

Of the holdings only 4 farmers or 'Yeoman' as they were called, had over 100 acres, 7 had 50 acres; 9 between 30–50 acres; another 9 between 20 and 30 acres; 6 had between 10 and 20 acres. The commons were described as 'very bad ground', and were the high moors to the North East, still pretty bleak today.

Even though the farmers were for the most part independent they had, at times, to combine their forces. The old system was communal, the harvest was cut with sickles, the scythe which cut close to the ground was not used as much as in Roman Times as the straw was not in such demand as on the later stock farms. Animals were slaughtered in the autumn because there was not enough food to keep them through the winter. Even in the 19th century in the prosperous mining days it took several people to harvest a field of corn, as the photo by Tom Page shows from Mr. T. Page's 'Photographs of Rosedale' published privately 1907, at Yatts Farm about ten are at work, men scything, boys 'woad' wappin or making straw bands or carrying sheaves, women and girls did the latter tasks. Haytime needed the same force turning, raking up and making hay-cocks or 'pikes', especially in a 'Catchy' time. The staple food of the dalesfolk in the Middle Ages was porridge of oatmeal, soups of peas or beans, flat cakes or small loaves of rye or barley, or 'haver cakes' (bread wheat came later), bacon, sausage and fish were eaten, but meat was scarce, especially in winter and spring. Honey was valued, there was no sugar until the 17th century and it was also used to make mead, a very ancient drink as remains of it have been found in a Bronze Age bucket. In the Iron Age a kind of beer was brewed from barley flavoured with cranberry and bog-myrtle.

Turf and wood were for ages the main fuel, later moor coal filled the gap until Durham and West Riding coal came, first by pannier pack-horse, then by rail. The foresters allowed the dalefolk to collect dead wood for burning and live or greenwood for building (Housebote). Oaks from the forest of Pickering or Spaunton were allocated carefully and entered into the Duchy of Lancs. records. In 1495 we find: 'Item, The Prioress of Rosedale: 'Two payers of forks, two ribbes wall-plates and rafters'. . . . There are many similar entries showing the erection or rebuilding of the universal type of cruck-framed long house of time immemorial. They still survive, though all the best Rosedale examples were swept away by the mining boom and the resultant opening of quarries of good freestone. Even today traces of the cut-down cruck beams remain in several old buildings, often re-used as lintels for doors or windows. The fundamental cruck-frame was a couple of forks, or siles, as they are sometimes called, adzed oak tree trunks or branches with their natural curve, set on base stones, and raised in the 'A' formation held together by tie-beams, held on top by a ridge pole usually resting on a saddle. They were raised in 'bays' about 16 ft. apart, hence it was easy to add another set to form a long-house with animals housed under the same roof only divided from humans by a cross-passage running the full width of the house. This was used for threshing corn, hence the name 'threshold' for the entrance doorways; these doors were opened on a windy day whilst the flail men worked on the corn, the chaff was blown out at the opposite end. 'Truff oppen deears' was the local name for them. The roofs of these houses were thatched with rye-straw or heather, held to the rafters by straw bands and hazel rods.

The living end was called the 'firehouse'; at first the hearth was in the centre, smoke escaping through a hole in the roof, later by smokehood supported on a massive cross-tie beam. By the hearth was the 'high seat' very similar to those described in the Norse sagas, where the head of the household and his wife sat. On either side of the seat were twin posts or pillars, holding the canopy. These were carved with potent 'runes' or charms invoking the god Thor, protector of the home, whose sacred tree was rowan or mountain ash, also used for protection against witchcraft. With the advent of Christianity they were carved with a so-called St. Andrew's cross by the parish priest. With the use of chimney stacks the seat became the ingle-nook close by the fireplace held on one side by a single support now called the 'witch post' it was thought to prevent the evil influence of the witch from entering by the passage or chimney. Witchposts survived long in Cleveland and Ryedale, they can still be found in Farndale and Egton. The only Rosedale witch-post was removed for use as a gate stop from Low Bell End, a farmstead of the old type restored in the 18th century. The post was in its old position by the hearth until 1960. It has been given to the Ryedale Folk Museum and skilfully restored by Peter Cook and the Stang-End post can also be seen there in its original setting. At Glaisdale there is a dated example of 1664 with the initials of the owners. Another stands at the end of the partition, 'the

Mill Street – Rosedale Abbey 1923. These elegant and well built mid-Victorian houses have survived with little external alteration. The building on the left was the butcher's shop.

speer' screening the seat from the cross-passage, at Quarry Farm, Glaisdale, elaborately carved with projecting strips or 'billets'. These are replacements of much older posts for the belief in witchcraft was widespread; even today old folks will tell of witches who turned into hares or cats that could not be caught unless a silver bullet was shot at them, or a black hound loosed on them. Canon Atkinson and Fairfax Blakeborough had recorded much of this lore before radio and television ended the recital of folk-lore by the log or turf fires on a winter evening.

One of the famous Rosedale witches was Hester Wood who could use her evil eye with dire results and could turn into a cat when she wished. Ann Skelton of Pickering told the tale of a witch-held maid who was 'brought up over and anest the village of Rossdil'. Nanny Skaife of Spaunton Moor lived in a turf hut and had a wonderful recipe for making the magic cube to fortell coming events. No wonder the witch posts survived into the present times.

The cruck houses in the dale were almost all renovated or entirely rebuilt in the prosperous mining era, though there is the evidence at Heygate, farmed for over two hundred years by the Peirson family, of a dated stone there inscribed I.R.P. 1756. The house was thatched in the 19th century though the present cow-house was possibly the earlier dwelling. Pry Hill (now gone), like one near Thorgill where William Champion remembered three pairs of crucks in a ruined house and Venom's Nick, now almost destroyed, was a typical long-house. Stone Bank and the building to the east called 'Simpson House' from the man who lived there in the 19th century was another. Others of the 16th and 17th century type were old Hollins (Moorlands) rebuilt 1748, now a byre; High Gill with its fine lintel; Craven Garth rebuilt in the early part of the 20th century and Dyke House with its building containing a window from the Priory all show ancient origin.

Hall Farm West Side (SE 695982) The site was monastic property until the 16th century and there was probably a house here before the present one. The appearance of the 1716 house can be reconstructed. It was lower than at present and extended no further than the main building. A cross passage from the front door which has a chamfered frame with a pointed arch, on the lintel R. W.:1716 I.H., R.W. is also cut into a quoin under the thin skewed fire window of the living kitchen. East of this is the 'low end' with a second door up three steps and one window. A nice dog kennel is outside the window of the back kitchen. It was a large house for 1716, built by Robert Watson, his successor another Robert was in possession of the farm of 87 acres in 1838 when the tithe award was made, at that date it was probably called Ellers. By 1850 the eaves had been raised and windows altered, a new low end had been added, or converted from an outbuilding, with another cross-passage. More outbuildings had been added on the south side and an outshot on the rear. All this may have been the work of Thomas Dale, a Rosedale man, who aquired the property from the Watsons after 1836.

An extract from Thomas Dale's notebook gives the date of the lease 1753, time unexpired 561 years. Thomas Watson sold it to his son for 5/- in the reign of George II, at a peppercorn rent. It was later sold at Castleton in 1879 for £3,000. Much of the old timber was removed in the 19th century though re-used upper crucks remain in the low end and a lintel over the low door at the east end, also other pieces of cruck timber with peg-holes. Like most dale houses it has a stream running at the rear utilized for many purposes including a water-wheel for generating electricity.

The farm is now a stock farm from 1960, the house is abandoned but the land managed from Kirkbymoorside. It is an example of the economic and structural changes of the past two centuries, (the house was surveyed in 1977 by members of the North Yorkshire and Cleveland Vernacular Building Study Group from which the notes were taken).

The Milburn Arms was also a reconstruction of the long-house, in the 1850 survey it is called 'The Hall', sometimes 'Varden Hall' from the squire of the time; the residence of a substanial family when it was renovated in the 18th century. On a keystone carved like an open book, there is an allusion to the Page family – 17 JOHN PAGE 76. The Garbutts kept house here when it was then called The Crown Inn. It retains much old timberwork including the sawn off ends of the great hearth beam in which the former smoke-hood rested. The Garbutts later removed to the White Horse, a mining foundation which, in 1840 was a farm called Lane Head. In the prosperous days of the late 19th century it was said more beer ran under its back door than is now consumed inside! Hartoft End, former 'Traveller's Rest' was kept by the Pennock's for many years, it was popular with the miners for a Sunday walk out and back, or for a cycle run calling at other inns on the way. There was a Black Cock Inn kept by William Wilson in Hartoft where other congregations gathered to hear a sermon by Mr. R. Foster of Pickering in 1856. Beer houses existed in Thorgill and at Red Barn in Northdale, the latter on an old road to Guisborough. Hamer House stood in solitary state on the moorland road to Egton Bridge, 1,100 ft. above sea level, a shelter for storm-bound travellers, Joe Ford was born there, and remembered his father coming home in a blizzard almost entirely covered by snow and ice. The last inhabitants were the Boddy family until the 1930s, since then it gradually fell to ruin. In the 18th century it had a neighbour in the Gibson house to the north, now only turf walls of its intake are visible; to the east was Turnhill, now a byre. The standing stone there was one of Peter de Mauley's boundaries in the 14th century. High Hamer, now a barn and sheep house, retains its salt box and housed 7 families in the 19th century.

In Hartoft, the group of farms around Wind Hill (possibly from Wand Hill, the first staked-out field) could be very early settlements; flints and bee-hive type querns came from this area. Near Birch House traces of rigg and furrow can be seen; on a corbel on this house is IR 1671 T.P., below I.P.H., 1804, the latter standing for Isaac and Penelope Harland, ancestors of a branch of the Cropton Harlands.

Two small fields in Hartoft were called 'Court Fields' and there is 'Court Bank' not far away, indicating that the open air court was held there in medieval times.

In 1670 Thomas Boyes and Eliza, his wife, were letting or selling Muffles Farm to John Atkinson; in 1627 a Gilbert Boies de Rosdela and William his son are mentioned. This family hailed from Lockton where they were hereditary foresters and the name is Norman–French for 'Wood-man'.

Northdale a hundred years ago had nine farms in occupation to the present two. The main farm on the east side has grown from a group of detached buildings to a large courtyard type. Hanging Stone House is now a ruin, it has groove stones for skellbeast partitions for cow-stalls, and may be a rebuilding of an early long-house.

Southfield, uninhabited since 1946, had stone pens for ducks and geese; Hither House, where the old track crossed the valley, has entirely vanished. Higher up there were small cottage holdings, one called Ebenezer was later the home of a retired miner J. Spenceley, who cut out a huge natural rock into pens for pigs and poultry, the rock is 20 ft. long and 3–4 ft. high, the pens 3 ft. by 2 ft. and 3 ft. by 5 ft., with two more even smaller ones; all have solid rock floors and grooves for wooden sliding panels with holes for iron bars. It was roofed with timber or metal sheets. Mr Fred Hall who first pointed out the nature of this relic has saved future archaeologists a lot of research for it resembles a neolithic rock-cut tomb in the Orkneys called the 'Dwarfie Stone'. West Northdale was the Suggett's farm of the 1649 survey. Above Red Barn on High Northdale Head, are traces of old fields now grown back to moorland, to the North East is Job's Well a petrifying spring of chaleybeate. Otter Hills below the Knott has gone, kennels are shown there on the 1914 map, the otter was mercilessly hunted in the last century and is now almost exterminated. Much stone was quarried here in the mining days.

A schoolmaster in Rosedale (Hodgson) is first mentioned in 1740, he may have run a private school on the west side as he was buried at Lastingham. T. Hall ran another in 1800, and by 1856 there was a 'Free School' on the site of the present shop and post office. Other private schools flourished in the boom period. Thomas Peirson of Heygate who died in 1720, left £5 per year from Dale Head farm (west side) and from a farm in Bransdale to provide free education for three children from Rosedale East and two from Hartoft. Later it was spent on prizes for them.

The Quakers had a hold in the dale, though there are few records of them. In 1604 William Turner and William Dobson (tailor) did not receive communion, in 1658 Robert Pearson of Rosedale spent 20 weeks in Pickering castle, and later was heavily fined for non-payment of tithes. William Wilkinson of Rosedale died while in prison. Gregory Pierson and other 'Friends in Blakemore in Cleveland' were fined a total of £167/19/-.

Archbishop Herring's visitation in 1720 records (by the curate C. J. Turner) under Rosedale Chappel Rydal:

> 'The number of inhabitants are about 50, the few dissenters we have are Quakers'
> 'We have no licensed meeting house within our chappelry'
> 'We have a small charity school, at the dower of the endowment; as many childern are taught as £5 amounts to'

The rest is mainly church details, they had 90 people at Easter Communion; the curate resided at Danby, 'the journey over the moor makes it troublesome, so we have only fortnightly service in winter'. It was signed by Edward Dowson, John Peirson, Robert Watson and William Frank. The methodist preacher, John Castillo, the 'Bard of the Dales', was in Rosedale in 1838; he wrote that he preached three times, 'several wept, but none

The Shepherds Retreat Club, or Ancient Order of Shepherds, a kind of friendly society held regular meetings, with an annual walk ending in a procession to church and dinner.

Blakey Junction c.1890. The train is about to leave for Incline Top. The Rosedale branch east is diverging on the right. The goods sidings and railway cottages are on the left.

High Shop – Rosedale East. 1908–10?

fairly yielded' and later, 'Rosedale was not awake to the cause of God'. Two of his poems are on Rosedale Festival, an event of which he evidently did not approve. 'More like a fair than a festival' he remarks. It was held in the churchyard if fine, inside the church if wet. Lasses and lads went there in large numbers, there was 'a vast of music', bands and anthems, but on the other hand lads fought for girls and much ale was consumed.

'Two rustics I shall touch upon
wi' ankle boots and leggins on,
Got sadly drunk, as I heard tell
And fought at Rosedale Festival:
They ate all Tommy Peirson's pie
And drank Jack Dowson's cellar dry,
And had to go to't Abbey well
to quench their thirst at't festival:'

He goes on to write about the fairer side, though this is a rather pious elegy in Victorian style, like his 'Rosedale Bob and Hartoft John' only the last verse dwells on the subject:

'Theres Jimmy Petch, as faithful as the dial,
And Tommy Peirson manges the viol;
Ephriam and Dowson high their voices raise
And Bob-at-Clough, he thunders in the bass':

The Methodists flourished exceedingly later, building three chapels and another at Thorgill.

The Shepherds Retreat Club, or Ancient Order of Shepherds, a kind friendly society, held regular meetings, with an annual walk, ending in a church or chapel service, and a dinner. They were headed by the brass band, though in 1869 by one from Lastingham. Rosedale had one by 1830; by 1850 they also had a 'Blue Ribbon' or Temperance band.

In the mining days there were plenty of musicians, the Champion family produced several; Jonathan Champion was a notable conductor of bands and chapel anniversaries, he made Farndale Silver Band famous in the period 1910–40.

What would Castillo have thought of the goings-on in September 1856, when a 'Gipsy Party' was held under the able direction of Messrs. Page, Pybus, Thorley and Snowdon. Three hundred people watched a cricket match between Rosedale and Wrelton and after a 'high tea', dancing commenced at 5 p.m., on the green to the strains of the brass band. This carried on until the shades of evening caused the party to retire to Mr. Maw's large room, where a merry dance and gipsy revelry was kept up to a late hour!

But that was not enough for the hearty dalesfolk for next day, as there was a quantity of 'good things' left over, they organized a treat for no less than 100 'matronly females' who enjoyed themselves immensely with tea and a 'feast of fat things'. Later they again withdrew to Mr. Maw's large room to trip the 'light fantastic'.

In 1858 the local newspaper reported 'Rosedale is one of the most beautiful and romantic vales in the north of England, the ivy-covered ruins of the abbey that had withstood the blasts of 600 years, looked down on a charming scene of dancers on the green all whirling to the strains of the Quadrille Band lead by Mr. Pybus. Little did the writer know the blast that was to destroy the abbey was not far distant.

As well as all this festivity there were horse and donkey races, foot races and hound trials – despite long hours and hard work these Victorians enjoyed themselves.

Even during the hard-up days of the strikes and closure of the mines in the 1920–30s there were lively dances held in the Lecture Hall. I well remember seeing it full of dancers with a Cleveland Dance Band playing the 'Ideal Schottische' and the Eva Three-Step; all moving in perfect rythmn and timing.

But Victorian times had its dark days for large families, living in overcrowded conditions, led to disease, in April 1869 typhus fever raged in the dale, 4 or 5 people died and over 50 were affected. Accidents in the mines or on the railway were numerous.

The population rose rapidly in the mining era, from 558 in 1851, to 2,839 in 1871, declining to 702 in 1881 after a recession, then rising to 1,396 in 1901, (possibly nearer 5,000 with lodging miners), falling to 962 in 1931, and to 286 in 1961. Rosedale West lost most in the past 35 years, no less than 200.

It was in Victorian times that the trade in jet ornaments reached its peak. The Queen set the fashion, the nation followed. Jet was mined extensively in the dales, scars and workings follow the band of lias shale. Little is known of the method of local workings, apart from the fact it was a 'chancy' business, some were lucky, others toiled in vain on the same levels. In Rosedale it was mined at the 'Heads' an oval hill, 675 ft., south of Craven Garth and Hill Cottages, also nearby below School Row, and in the Dale Head below Cat Nab Scar. All these workings must have taken place after 1848 as they are not shown on the first edition of the O.S. map. Other workings were in Northdale, where in 1856, T. Page says one Whitby jet worker made £500 from Northdale jet. 'Jet is worked to great advantage' and it was classed with iron ore to boost the proposed railway line. In Thorgill remains of jet holes were pointed out to me by the Drings, opposite Gill Bank. They were probably run by miners in periods of depression in the iron stone industry, for by the 1880s trade was declining. Moor coal mining was a much older trade, possibly even going back to Roman Times. One of the first records is from Helmsley Castle in 1070 AD. By the 17th–18th centuries many dalesmen had their own pits, like Coalpit ridge at Hartoft End (late 16th century) and around the Dale Head, especially at Blakey where early inn-keepers were recorded as 'Colliers' in burial registers. Another large coalfield was around Hamer House, while the name 'Coal Pit Hill' in Northdale speaks for itself. The Rosedale coal was traded for lime-burning at Cropton and south of Hutton-le-Hole, where it was used extensively in the kilns. With wood or peat and turf it could be used on the open hearths of the farmsteads. The last reported use of moor coal was during the 1926 general strike when miners opened shallow pits near Reeking Gill.

Jet workshop in Whitby. Photo courtesy of Whitby Literary and Philosophical Society.

XIII
The Ironstone Industry

We have already suggested that Rosedale iron was in use at a very early date and noted the mediaeval record of the 12th–13th century. A further mediaeval grant from St. Mary's Abbey to an iron founder in Rosedale West gives some interesting details. Dated August 1339, it entitles, 'John, son of Richard, the chief smithyman' lease to occupy a plot of land within the Abbot's forest of Rosedale, to take fuel from the woods by permission of his foresters, to smelt and make profit from iron-ore'. He was allowed to pasture seven horses on the common; but had to deliver 16 stones of iron per week to the bailiff at Spaunton Manor, though if he found ore before Christmas he had to produce 18 stones at Spaunton. This sounds rather ambiguous, presumably his father, Richard, had bloomeries in blast already producing iron. At Spaunton the reheating forge was found at the west end of the medieval hall; many lumps of iron slag (imperfectly smelted according to a Cargo Fleet analysis) lay on the floor around the forge.

The site of the medieval Rosedale West Bloomery was found by Douglas Smith in 1974 opposite Hartoft End and excavated by local people under the direction of R.H.H. by 1978. There were several working sites, furnace remains of a small round furnace base 60 by 70 cms in diameter, reused several times. It was possibly blown by bellows through Tuyere holes. A large amount of slag lay on the east side in a trench leading up to the furnace. To the north was the pile of ore, obtained from the bank of the river a few metres away. Another large slag heap lay further to the north east on the bank of the Seven with traces of further hearths and a U-shaped enclosure consisting mainly of slag and stones. This had pottery of the 15th–16th century in the banks though the pottery near the furnace and roasting hearth 'D' was 14th century, confirmed by the find of a coin of Edward I. 1309, minted at Canterbury.

This confirms the documentary evidence of John, son of Richard, the chief smithyman handing over the site to his son in 1339. A report of this interesting early ironworking industry is forthcoming. It shows the persistence of the Iron Age type of furnace very similar to that on Levisham Moor into the 14th century over 1200 years. A similar bloomery was dug out on Postgate Hill in Glaisdale by George Harland. It was 8 ft. long by 3 ft. wide and sunk into the rocky hillside 3 ft. down. In it was a mass of run slag and some potsherds of the period. It was worked by bellows, no waterpower being available. Other similar sites have been excavated in Danby and Baysdale.

These small bloomeries all ceased to work by the 18th century; William Marshall in 1780 said: 'no ironworking taking place at present apart from Forge Valley, in the dales the remains of old furnaces can be seen'. The most prosperous era of Rosedale iron-ore began in 1855 with open-cast quarrying into a deep, though narrow, boat-shaped trough of magnetic ore at the base of the Dogger, to below the level of green mud-stone. The great nugget of iron projected like a cliff over the daleside. This was called the Kitchen-Garbutt deposit; it lay on the west side of the dale above Hollins Farm, a huge scar in the shale marks the site. It was stated later that 'Rosedale has lately sprung into notice through the discovery of an extensive deposit of ironstone, highly magnetic, yields a large percentage of metal, the vein is about 18ft. in thickness and easily worked by drifts'. In 1856 a lease was given by Thomas Garbutt to George Leeman (Deputy Chairman of the North Eastern Railway), Isaac Hartas and Alexander Clunes Sheriff.

The ore was taken by horse-drawn waggons to Pickering, then by rail to various ironworks, including the Derwent Works, Consett. A letter published in the Malton Messenger in February 1856 gives some idea of the difficulty of road transport at this time: 'the road from Cropton to Hartoft Bridge is a complete bog from end to end, full of clay holes, many 2 ft. deep, almost impossible for waggons with a load without being broken to pieces. I noticed a waggon laden with iron ore, no less than eight horses yoked to it to drag it through the mire. The road further on to Rosedale is even worse'. Even so 3 to 4,000 tons of ore were taken to Pickering in the first 5 years. A proposed railway line was surveyed the same year, why it was eventually laid on the high moors with two dangerous inclines is a mystery, even at that time letters appeared urging that the line should run down Rosedale via Askew to Hutton and Douthwaite, 'where it is said ironstone is to be found in abundance and lead ore in the land of J. F.

Rosedale Chimney 1948. The engine-house chimney of the West Mines incline tramway built by Flintoft of Lastingham in 1860 and demolished in 1972. The chimney was a landmark for many miles. The railway reservoir is in the foreground.

Shepherd' (Douthwaite, this is doubtful). In October of the same year it is stated 'large numbers of labourers have been employed erecting a gin for sinking a shaft on the mountain range between Lastingham and Rosedale, so that ore can be conveyed to the top without an expensive incline'. This was probably at Sheriff's pit.

When the North Eastern Railway completed the Rosedale Branch in 1861, an incline tramway was built (in 1860) from the horizontal drifts of Hollins Mines to the terminus at Bank Top 1,000 ft. above sea level. The ore was sent up in rope-hauled waggons for half a mile, ascending 400 ft. to the large kilns (made at Jarrow), alongside the line.
The ore was tipped into the kilns from above and then 'roasted' to drive off water and carbonic acid gas, a process known as calcination. This reduced the weight of the ironstone, with a saving of costs, though the 'roasting' process involved the use of coal.
Moor coal was obtained at first from local pits, later it was all brought from Durham. Much of the masonry of the kilns remains, but the front shutters and other ironwork has gone. The line of the tramway is still clearly visible.
In November 1861 it was reported 'a large number of waggons were being drawn up the incline, when a coupling chain broke and the whole lot were seen rushing downwards with fearful rapidity, illuminating the line with fire, which in the darkness was truely awful. A man named Illingworth (alias Buttons) received a fractured collar bone and other injuries, but he is recovering'!

At Bank Top the buildings housing the stationary engine were ready for use by March 1861. Three large low pressure boilers of the Collings standing tube type, weighing two and a half tons each, were hauled from Pickering, via Hutton-le-Hole to Bank Top, by 40 horses and dozens of men pushing, and filing up holes in the muddy road. The tall chimney was built by John Flintoft of Lastingham, who was said to have danced on top of it when the task was finished. Rosedale Chimney was demolished by the landowner in July 1972, after standing as a landmark for 112 years. The reason for its great height was explained by the demand by Squire Darley, the land-owner, that the smoke should not upset his grouse!

The engine shed for the railway, as well as the row of 16 railwaymens' cottages, was completed in 1860–61. There were several accidents to workmen on the steep bank to the village with its 1 in 3 gradient, horses slipped and bolted with dire results.

In the first full year of operation, after the completion of the railway over 200,000 tons of ore were carried, this rose to nearly 300,000 tons in 1864. Maximum production was reached in 1872–4, under the management of J. Parking, but a strike of miners from May 11th to June 22nd 1874 brought a temporary closure and those who were not sacked had to return for lower wages. A recession in the industry brought a further period of closure in March 1879. A new company, West Rosedale Ironstone Co., was formed, but only continued working until the final shut-down in 1885. Since then the tall chimney ceased to smoke, its brief working life only 24 years – a landmark until 1972.

It was said the ironstone, in deposits 70 ft. thick, extending into the daleside for quarter of a mile were not fully worked out, others denied this statement, though hopes of a revival persisted until 1945.

Water was obtained by means of an open leat or cutting from the springs and marshes (Jewel Marsh) south of Thorgill. This was conducted into a reservoir, still visible, near the chimney. The Spaunton court jury of 1860 surveyed the course and imposed annual fines on the company. Mr. Garbutt, chief engineer, promised to make culverts over the leat and see that it was no more than 2 ft. in depth.

XIV
Sheriff's Pit — Rosedale West

West Mines about a mile north west of the hamlet of Thorgill were originally leased to a Mrs. Jane Spink in 1857, later they were worked by the Rosedale and Ferryhill Iron Co. Unlike the other mines it operated in a similar manner to a coal mine, the ore being raised to the surface through a vertical shaft sunk to the drift 270 ft. below, and discharging alongside the railway. Horizontal drifts were driven in at the outcrop on the daleside above Medd's Farm, at an altitude of 825 ft; one extended 1,500 ft. to the base of the vertical shaft. This was used as a tramway carrying the ore from a loading bay on a terrace at the entrance of the drifts. At the pit-head the ore was tipped directly into the trucks without the calcination process on the spot. The trade recession brought about a closure of these mines from 1879 to 1881.

Sheriff's Pit came under control of the Carlton Iron Co., shortly after the Rosedale East Estate passed into the hands of the present owners, the Milburn family, in 1879. Francis J. H. Lascelles became manager and lived in a substantial house by the shaft. The pit carried on operations until 1911 when difficulties of underground haulage and infiltration of water became too great. The seam varied from 8 ft. at the outcrop to 5 ft. where the work was abandoned, but the useable stone got narrower until the working place was only 80 yards wide when left, so indications were the ironstone was entirely vanishing. The gear was removed in 1911, and today only the great open shaft remains, with the ruins of the manager's house and a few foundations of the rest of the buildings by the abandoned line. Traces of a building and loading bay can be seen by the quarries and tips above Medd's Farm.

One of Rosedale's most outstanding characters William Champion first began his working career at Sheriff's Pit, he was born at an old thatched house called 'Clough' west of the Knott, on the east side of the dale and was one of a very large family. His mother was said to have had 22 children twice!, this came about by the fact she had 22 children, then one died before the 23rd was born. This was an age of large families and heavy infant mortality, but despite this several of them lived to a good age. William attended East side School, and at 13 left to take a waggoner's job at a Hartoft Farm. He left this (the wage was only £5 a year), to take on pumping and bailing water from the pit, always a problem at Sheriff's Pit. He also helped the blacksmith, taking a keen interest in this work and soon became 'Top Dog' at the princely salary of 4/- per day. He had a sharpening hut on the loading bay, where he sharpened and made tools for the pit, as well as shoeing all the 32 pits ponies, and forging pit-axes and hammers. When Sheriff closed he became head blacksmith at the East Mines, also engineer, at 5/- per day, working from 4 a.m. to 10 p.m., at times during the boom period of the 1914–18 war; sometimes he never went home and his meals were brought to his hut. He lived to the great age of 97 and in his last years could still talk lucidly of the days he spent in the mines. When he died in 1966, J. Fairfax Blakeborough wrote (In Whitby Gazette) 'He was the mechanical and engineering brain behind the working of the mine. With his genius he could have easily obtained a manager's position, or even a director's, but he chose to remain quiet and unassuming, even in the face of difficulties.'

Sheriff's Pit (1857–1911). The pit manager's house is on the left with stores and workshops in the centre of the photograph. The pit head gear was the only one of its type used in Rosedale and was similar to the gear used in coal mining districts. An open shaft and rubble foundations is all that remain today.

XV
East Mines

These workings appear to have started shortly after those of the west side, about 1859–60, by the same company, Rosedale and Ferryhill Iron Co., until they failed in 1879. Carlton Iron Co., took over with Lascelles, as manager until 1911 – the year Sheriff's Pit closed. They were re-opened the following year by Messrs. Lascelles and Shepherd and worked profitably during the first world war. In 1919 they were taken over by Messrs. J. Shepherd and H. Pringle, but their days were numbered as production costs rose and competition with low-priced foreign ores became acute. Finally they closed during the general strike of May 1926, never to re-open.

The bed or workable stone was 14ft.–16ft. thick, though the quality deteriorated until working became unprofitable. There was a narrow seam of magnetic stone; extensive workings went a distance of 3 miles into the hillside in horizontal drifts at an altitude of 925 ft. on the vale side. The drifts had 9 ft. headroom and were 12 ft. wide; open lamps and candles were used at first, no explosive gas being present, though foul air was always a danger. The square squat chimney still standing above the kilns at Low Baring acted as a ventilator, as did Jack Sharp's shaft near the Castleton Road. Water infiltration was a problem, pumps worked continually and if they stopped there was a three-quarter-mile-long syphon to drain out. Falls of shale and serpula sandstone were frequent, many accidents occurred as 100 men were employed on each shift. In severe weather, which was the rule up there in winter, men came out wet through to have their clothes and boots frozen. So that they had to be thawed or sometimes cut off.

In 1866, the first full year of operation, over 168,000 tons of ironstone were produced by East Mines, but this figure was doubled in the early 1870s. These were only maintained for a few years, and under the Carlton Iron Co., the figures were much less.

The ore waggons were originally horse-drawn; later one of the steam boilers

Sheriff's Pit had no electricity but East Mines had a generator installed in 1900 by Carlton Iron Co. The generator was dismantled in 1911 when the company ceased operation.

T. W. Ward's hopper for loading calcine dust at the 'Old Kilns', Rosedale East. 1927. Part of the kilns and ventilating shaft chimney can be seen in the background.

used at Bank Top to provide power to haul the waggons from Hollins mine, was re-used to haul waggons from the East Mines to large kilns alongside the North Eastern Railway line. These remain, an impressive monument to Victorian industry, their iron work gone, though the massive stonework still stands. There were two sets, the older nearer High Baring, the later half a mile north. Foundations of other buildings including dwelling houses, offices and sheds can be seen.

In 1900 an electric generating plant was installed, a remarkable innovation at this period, especially in view of the remoteness of the mine it was used for lighting, drilling, and haulage and was removed when the Carlton Iron Co., ceased operations in 1911.

The calicine dust piled in tips below the entrances of the mines as waste was removed when it was found later to be of commercial value, in 1926–29 by Messrs. T. W. Ward of Sheffield for processing at Middlesbrough. The last load was transported on January 11th, 1929.

In the early years of these mines the ironstone outcrop was extensively quarried from the Old Kilns and the Depots, to Knott Road and the edge of Northdale, as far as Bell End (or Top). A tramway followed the line of workings at 850 ft., the terrace and cuttings are still visible; it had a narrow gauge (3 ft.) and two 0-4-0 ST locos 'Rosedale' and 'Emily' were used to draw the waggons. Knott Road was carried over the line by a bridge, long ago replaced by an embankment. The tramway had a short life and was probably abandoned by 1879.

The only other working of the period was a drift mine called Blakey Mine, situated south of Blakey Bank on the Farndale slope. It was in a pocket of the Dogger seam, but was unprofitable, 'not enough iron to nail my boots' said a miner. Even so, it was run by R. Lavery & Co., from 1873 to 1895, and a spur of railway line three-quarters of a mile long connected its tramway incline to the main line at Blakey Junction. Remains of this can still be traced on the moor.

The population rose to its peak of almost 3,000 in the 1870s. Many more crowded into lodgings, others lived in the surrounding villages and walked or rode on horses or donkeys to the pits, often struggling with atrocious weather conditions.

Rows of plain though substantial cottages were built for the miners at Rosedale Abbey, Thorgill, Low and High Row while near East Mines were

Miners at a drift entrance above Medds Farm, Thorgill c.1900. One of these drifts extended to the foot of Sheriff's Pit, a distance of about 1500 ft.

East Mines calcining kilns.

High Baring, Florence Terrace, Hill Cottages and School Row.

Other houses were renovated to accommodate lodgers, such as High Gill and Bell End, while at Low Bell End old farm buildings were converted into cottages, also another group at Heygate. High and Low Row, most of Florence Terrace, and several others have gone, including the railway cottages at Bank Top, but School Row, Hill Cottages and some at Thorgill remain. Douglas Smith surveyed several turf-built structures called 'Irishman's Huts' situated in Rosedale Head at NZ 686006, between Cat Nab Scar and Green Head Brow at over 1000 ft. above sea level. Foundations of seven buildings – 6 measured 28 by 5 m with a seventh 12 by 75 m. They were railway navvies' temporary huts used between 1864 and the line opening on August 18th, 1865.

The mines and railway are fully described with several illustrations in Scarborough and District Archaeological Society's Report No. 9, 1974.

Many of the miners and navvies were Irish, Scots or Negroes. Fierce disputes and brawls broke out; pitched battles between the Irish and other groups are recorded. On one occasion the police bundled the whole lot into a covered waggon and took them to Pickering to 'cool their heels' for a couple of days in the jailhouse.

But on the whole, despite hard conditions they were a fairly cheerful and hospitable crowd and food was plain, though cheap and plentiful. The little community known as Rosedale Abbey, around the site of the Priory, remained the only real village in the dale. As well as the rows of cottages there were shops, joiners, cobblers, and other tradesmen. The Rosedale and Ferryhill Iron Co., built the lecture hall, with a schoolroom above in 1873; soon afterwards it was turned into a temporary hospital because so many miners were involved in accidents. The church was rebuilt on the site of the conventual chapel, other buildings included two Methodist chapels and the Crown Inn, a favourite centre for sportsmen and pleasure parties and well patronised even in the early part of the 19th century. It became the Milburn Arms in 1958.

Rosedale East was included in the parish, it had the various groups of miners' dwellings below the 'Depots' and East Mines. There was a shop, various tradesmen, a Methodist Chapel and a school was also established. Rosedale West had no village, scattered communities existed at Bank Top, Lann Head, around the White Horse Inn, Low and High Rows, and at

Thorgill which was a small hamlet around a shop, chapel and mill, though it was originally based on a tiny group of farms.

Hartoft was always a scattered farming community, but earlier traces of industry are found there.

Only four houses on the far left remain of this once substantial terrace. The stone for building was of local origin but the roofing slate was transported in, usually from Wales.

XVI
The Railway

In 1858 the N. Yorks, and Cleveland railway extended its line to Ingleby, Battersby and Kildale. Battersby Station, originally Ingleby Junction became Battersby Junction though the name was shortened to Battersby in 1893. The company was soon absorbed by the North Eastern Railway, which also took over a narrow gauge line from Battersby to Rudd Scar Iron mine at the foot of Ingleby Incline. This was relaid as a single standard gauge track, later extended by the incline to Rosedale Bank Top a distance of 14 miles and opened on March 27th 1861.

At Battersby there were marshalling sidings with a three-road engine shed for the Rosedale branch, which extended southwards in a direct line for two miles to the foot of the incline at 650 ft. There were sidings and several buildings here, including a weigh-house of which traces remain.

The new incline installed by the North Eastern Railway replaced the original one to the Rudd Scar Mines. It was about one mile in length ascending to moor top at 1,370 ft., on a gradient which commenced at 1 in 9, but eventually attained a maximum of 1 in 5. Waggons were hauled by steel ropes 1,650 yards long passing round 14 ft. drums. The descending loaded waggons, three or four at a time pulled up a set of empty waggons. The journey took three minutes at a speed of 20 m.p.h. Except for a short length at the foot, double tracks were in use on the incline with sidings to divert runaway waggons, a necessary precaution, as accidents were not infrequent despite extreme care in operation. One can imagine the fate of runaway waggons on a slope of 1 in 5!

From Incline Top the line kept on the high moors never below an altitude of 1,000 ft. for over eleven miles. It avoided the steep dale heads by means of numerous curves. Easy gradients were maintained and expensive viaducts made unnecessary by following the contours; cuttings and embankments were numerous, some of the latter at the dale heads being of substantial

With a maximum gradient of 1 in 5 the Ingleby Incline was the scene of a number of accidents. The normal rate of descent was 20 m.p.h. and the journey took three minutes.

Banktop—The N.E.R. Terminus (1000 ft. above Sea Level)

West Rosedale Bank Top c.1900. Stones from the engine shed on the left were used to build Hutton Village Hall 1938–9. The snowplough is on sidings which formerly extended to the calcining kilns at Bank Top. Only one of the cottages on the right still remains.

The staff of the L.N.E.R. at Incline top, August 3rd 1928. The guard stands on the left with the stoker and foreman third and fourth from left. The engine driver sits front left and the drum operator front right.

proportions. Shortly after leaving Incline Top the line crossed the watershed of the North York Moors by a shallow cutting which was a notorious snow trap and was provided with a hut, housing shovels and other equipment. Half a mile further on was Blowath Crossing, a lonely outpost on the rough road leading from Kirkbymoorside to Stokesley. It is little used today but in the earlier centuries a packhorse pannier-way joined it here and waggons followed the rigg route N-S. The gates remain but the cottage was destroyed during the 1939–45 war.

Two great loops carried the line around the twin heads of Farndale, then over a long embankment at Eskletts. At a point near the 8th milepost are the remains of a brick-built water tower supplied by two small reservoirs from nearby springs. A further great loop avoided Blakey Gill, an embankment carrying the line over Gill Wath and a slight rise to Blakey Bridge and Junction.

There was a little colony of railwaymen at Little Blakey living in a row of cottages by the line junction, with four other houses in a square behind and another three-storied house by the bank into Farndale.

The Castleton-Hutton road was carried over the line cutting by a stone bridge, the only example on the branch. Road improvements in 1954 converted the by-road into a busy highway, which is shrouded in fog or blocked by snow many days of the year. The cutting was another notorious snow-trap and three engines were used, two pushing the snow-plough the other reversed to pull them out if they stuck.

In January 1861 work on this section of the line was held up for three weeks, 40 labourers were caught in a sudden blizzard, the snowploughs could not reach then and they took refuge in temporary huts at Eskletts, near the water tower. A Mr. King, one of the railway officials, and the local constable, set out with shovels and food in search of them. They found the Eskletts huts completely buried under huge drifts and feared for the safety of the men; not a door or window was visible, but they succeeded in rescuing them with much digging. The men were almost exhausted having used up all food and fuel.

The original line from Blakey junction extended Southeastwards for about four miles, passing Sled Shoe House (now gone) and another pumping station in the form of a large metal pump on the line side.

At the 12th mile post was Sheriff's Pit with sidings and many buildings. The terminus was Bank Top, where a substantial two-road engine shed was erected in 1861, enlarged in 1863, and demolished in 1937–8, the stones being used to build the village hall at Hutton-le-Hole.

Sidings led to the Hutton road where a loading bay was erected and also to the kilns and incline to Hollins Mine. Water was obtained by the leat already mentioned.

The 16 cottages housed railwaymen and from 1926 they gradually decayed and were handed back to the Darley Estate at the closure. One was in use as a Youth Hostel from 1933 until 1950, now only two remain. Willie Wood, the last of the railway workers, lived here at No. 16 until his death in 1963, he was always ready to tell of the last days of the line.

Bank Top was the scene of the opening ceremony of the line on March 27th, 1861, when in the words of the Malton Messenger:-

> 'At 3 p.m. the engine, a most powerful one, with a train of waggons containing directors, engineers, and contractors, arrived at the terminus. Considering the weather of this wild district, the treacherous condition of the moors the line traverses; the early opening has conferred great credit to Messrs. Cail & Town the contractors. The workers were regaled on old English beef, bread, and ale.'

Amongst the many set-backs was a riot by men employed on building the Ingleby Incline, for the previous year on February 26th, 1860, the same newspaper reported:-

> 'Navvies, over 60 in number were in the pub of Mr. Sturdy helping themselves to liquor and victuals, some carried heavy bludgeons, when Mr. T. Towns, one of the contractors appeared with the men's wages apparently they received part in provisions, and one man, Plathook, said he would have nothing but cash. He struck at Mr. Sturdy with his staff and others set on Mr. Towns, who was knocked onto the floor bleeding and shouting "murder".'

Hill Cottage. Rosedale.

XVII
The East Branch

A single track to serve the East Mines was opened for traffic on August 18th, 1865 by the North Eastern Railway though its construction may have been commenced by the proprietors of the mines. The entire route of four-and-three-quarter miles follows the head of Rosedale, on a falling gradient almost to the mines. Entry involved a reversal of trains at Blakey Junction. The first one and a half miles run northwards to the dale head passing below Lion Inn, the isolated public house, still serving travellers on the high rigg road. Near the first mile post is a brick-built ruin, the remains of a water-tank fed by leats from a small reservoir. The line swings round dalehead by a high embankment over a stone culvert, to a deep cutting and another high embankment over Reeking Gill with a loop at Nab Scar. It continued to Black House, a linesman's cottage, dividing into spurs, one on a higher level to the mine entrances at High Baring, the other passing the 'new' kilns and on past the 'old' kilns to the terminus and goods 'Depot' via cottages and a goods shed (still used by a farmer), with coal staithes nearby at Depot Cottage, a whitewashed house that is still occupied. From here the 1870 tramway continued to Bell Top.

XVIII
Operation

During the peak period 1870–77 the Rosedale branch carried a daily average of 1,000 tons or more of iron ore, and night work was found necessary to cope with the high volume of traffic. The maximum load appears to have been 15 loaded waggons or 30 empty. Incoming traffic was light, but included coal, food fertilizers, timber, and oil, while some farm produce was carried to Battersby.

No passenger coaches were used, but passengers issued with passes, chiefly railwaymen or their families, were carried in the brake-van on the section above Ingleby Incline. They had to walk down the incline and transfer to ordinary passenger trains at Battersby. School children were also carried, from the cottages at Incline Top and Blowath to Blakey where they walked down the bank to Farndale school carrying their 'grub' in tin boxes as they had to lodge in Farndale until the train on Friday afternoon took them home.

The line was unfenced, only sheep strayed on the high moors and it was cheaper to compensate the owners than provide fences, particularly as it is unlikely that all the accidents were reported. Sounding the whistle and pelting with coal was the usual method of dislodging sheep which had a habit of sleeping on the track. Grouse and rabbits also suffered; one engine driver Jacob Baker was known to stop a train if there was a chance of catching game. On one occasion a linesman, finding a very dead grouse set it in view of the line as the train approached. What Jacob said is unprintable.

The line was unsignalled, a simple staff system control being used with a control point at Blakey Junction. A telephone line followed the entire route although it was often brought down by gales or snow. Brake vans and empty waggons were allowed to coast downhill from Blakey to the East Mines.

Normally five 0-6-0 tender engines were employed above the incline and housed at Bank Top Shed. At the end of the line these engines belonged to

Hand cutting by miners and railway men at Blakey Bridge. 1900. The signal cabin, platelayers hut and railway cottages at Little Blakey can be seen in the background. In 1893 the line was blocked for three months.

the N.E. Class P. (L.N.E.R. Class J 24); the last of which No. 1893, was lowered down the incline in 1929. Battersby engine shed held 9 locomotives, also six-coupled tender class.

Owing to the difficulty of lowering engines down the incline repairs were usually undertaken at the Bank Top shed. When major overhauls became necessary the locomotives' centre wheels were removed at the shed and the engine towed to Incline Top. To offset the severe conditions tender windscreens were fitted to all engines and tarpaulins frequently added. Derailments were overcome by means of lifting jacks, and improvisation was often responsible for keeping the traffic moving.

According to Mr. J. W. Featherstone, formerly of Battersby, who was in charge of the Ingleby Incline during the last years of its operation, the life of the railway workers and their families living on the exposed edge of the moorland 1,350 ft. above sea level without shelter from the West-North gales was hard, especially in winter. All the same they were a friendly and happy community, often joined by friends from Blowarth in gatherings and musical evenings of a type fast vanishing. Incline Top had the ironic nickname 'Siberia' but they had the consolation of quick and easy transport to Middlesbrough whenever they wished to go, but the walk back up the incline 'took the jam off it' as someone said. At Bank Top the railwaymen had to face an even steeper climb from the village inns or shops, 500 ft. up the notorious Rosedale Bank with a section 1 in 3.

They could also join the Mutual Improvement Society, which held meetings and lectures at the hall, or the brass, or the string band under Thomas Peirson; or they could join the festivity at the numerous concerts and dances.

Probably the chief enemy was the weather, winters could be very severe and lasted long on the high moors. In 1878/9 the snow began in November and ending with a thaw in February. In 1882 the line was completely blocked by a single snowstorm on December 2nd which lay until well into February.

The worst winter in the whole history of the line was that of early 1895. It began with a blizzard on the last day of December 1894. All roads were blocked by January 2nd, even the train from Pickering to York was snowed up in Lund cutting at Kirkbymoorside.

On the Tuesday following, a party of miners living at Lastingham tried to get to work at the Sheriff Pit, after toiling three miles up to their waists they had to give up the attempt and return. One Willie Gibb was lost in the driving drifts 'stouring' was the word used, he was found exhausted on Rosedale Bank Top by other miners, six hours later. By January 19th a road was opened from Hutton, but the line was still blocked and gangs of men were sent to dig it out; meanwhile the pits were on short time.

Blakey Junction just recovering from the first blizzard was struck by a second on January 13th, even more violent. Snow piled up in fantastic drifts, some houses were almost buried. By January 21st upwards of 100 men were employed cutting snow in a fruitless attempt to open the line, which was entirely submerged under 20 ft. drifts. On that day four horses were harnessed to a large sledge in an attempt to get to Pickering for a load of flour. This was also abandoned, food was scarce and stock suffering, hundreds of moor sheep were lost under the huge drifts. By February, East Mines were entirely closed by the snow, the postman who drove a mail cart from Pickering only got to Cropton Lane before he had to leave the cart and continue on horseback. Even after changing horses in the dale it took him 5–6 hours to do the round, a local man had to take over several times.

February was even worse, as well as deep snow, between the blizzards were spells of intense cold, frost recorded at Malton was 30 and even 40 degrees. Malton Messenger records 'William Cooper of Aislaby Hall generously provided 2 large waggon loads of coal, drawn by 4 horses they proceeded to Rosedale the road dug by gangs of men, as they went up the dale. Some idea of the suffering could be gained by the sight of men, women, and children dragging little sledges, others carrying the coal on their backs for distances of 3 miles, in some cases uphill.' Two men hauled a sledge to and from Glaisdale station for 1 cwt. of coal.

At Lastingham 200 grouse appeared in the village street driven by cold and hunger from the snow-covered feeding grounds.

Soup kitchens were opened at Rosedale Abbey by W. J. Mayman and H. Champion, 90 quarts of soup were given to 58 families and 58 loaves of bread with it. Soup kitchens were organized at Lastingham by the Vicar, Rev. J. S. Salmon, and at Hutton by J. F. Shepherd of Douthwaite Hall.

There was no thaw to speak of until March 19th, and it was mid-April before the line was opened and drifts remained in the cuttings until mid-June. A drought followed the severe winter and grouse were observed drinking from the melting snow in the cuttings. At Sheriff's Pit a huge pile of ironstone

Most of the original railway line ran at 1000 ft. or more for 14 miles. Severe winters piled up drifts like this in several cuttings and under Blakey Bridge. Hand cutting was the last resort when other engines had failed to pull or push a stranded train clear.

awaited the re-opening of the line. It was August before it was all removed, and a yard thickness of black snow was found underneath.

On February 22nd, 1900 a violent blizzard struck the Cleveland moors piling up 12 ft. drifts. Several carts stuck on the way to Rosedale and women and children were rescued from them and taken to nearby farms, while 20 men were cutting snow the postman got stuck in a drift, his horse firmly embedded up to the saddle and some of the men had to dig him out. It took him 4 hours and 4 fresh horses to get to the Abbey. During World War 1 the winter of 1916/17 brought the line to a standstill for 5 weeks. Heavy and persistent snowfalls resulted in drifts 30 ft. deep early in January, and the line was not re-opened until 12th February. Conditions at Blakey and Incline Top were particularly difficult with engines completely buried. A train returning from the Incline was trapped by drifting snow at Farndale Head with a woman passenger in the brake van. The crew and passenger were rescued by linesmen the following morning after they had taken refuge at Eskletts in Westerdale. Snow was still 4 ft. deep in places on April 17th.

Even the last winter of the line proved severe, for in February 1929, during the dismantling period, conditions were made difficult by strong freezing winds. According to Willie Wood, the whistle of a loco in steam at Blakey Junction was frozen.

Some idea of snow conditions on the high moors can be obtained by a report in the Malton Messenger, June 9th 1860, 'on May 28th a violent hurricane blew for 5 hours, snow fell heavily, drifting in places to a depth of 7 ft. On June 3rd many hedges and walls were completely covered, and all traffic stopped, while a road was cut through.'

Gales of this type provided an additional hazard and waggons were blown over the top of the incline. The worst gale in memory occurred on October 11th, 1881, and caused considerable damage in North East Yorkshire. A whirlwind, accompanied by thunder, damaged cottages at Bank Top in 1895.

XIX
The End of the Line

The decline of ironstone production after the First World War brought about a serious reduction of traffic on the branch; from four or more trains each way the number dwindled to one. Shortly after the final closure of the mines in 1926, the L.N.E.R. decided to abandon the line. During the 65 years of operation the branch carried about ten million tons of ironstone; over half in the first 17 years. Waste product of the calcining kilns was found to be valuable, so the closure was delayed until the great tips below the kilns were removed. This was completed in January 1929, and all the previous year T. W. Ward of Sheffield had the dismantling of the line and the removal of the waste tips in hand. The salvaged materials were sent down the incline and on June 8th, 1929, the last load was transported and the line declared closed on the 13th June. This was the final blow to the hopes expressed in the 1850s that the mining boom and the railway would last hundreds of years. In fact the end of the Cleveland mining industry was not far distant, the closure of Skelton Pit in 1964 ended an era that had lasted over 2,000 years since the little furnace was built on Levisham Moor, probably before the Romans came into Yorkshire. In the words of a director of Dorman Long & Co., 'it is finished irrevocably now.' There was only one other attempt to link Rosedale by rail in the 20th century. This was a proposal for a light railway on a standard gauge of 4 ft. 8 ins. for a distance of 8 miles to the North Eastern Railway branch at Sinnington. It was promoted by a Mr. Frederick Pope of Lastingham with local support. The route via the Seven Valley with a station near Askew for Lastingham, was surveyed in 1897 by Myers-Beswick of Leeds and the order was granted by the Railway Commissioners in October 1899.

The local paper reported on the news of this coming to Lastingham:-

> 'there was much excitement and rejoicing by many who were not affected by clerical and other influences (apparently the vicar was an

From Rosedale the railway ran along the moor top before descending the 1430 yard long Ingleby Incline. When the mines finally closed the engines were lowered down the incline, the last descent being on 8th June 1929.

> opponent of the scheme). On Friday afternoon a steam thrashing machine was driven up Listy Hill, with the men in a state of high jocularity, they attached an empty waggon to the machine exclaiming they would supersede "the Pope and his light railway". A steam whistle blew, amid roars of laughter they shouted "All change for Spaunton" as the engine puffed its way up the hill.'

Construction of the railway appears to have got as far as a sod-cutting ceremony at Rosedale Abbey on June 14th, 1902. Messrs. D. Milburn and T. Muncaster (the agent) were present and Capt. Darley was heard to remark afterwards 'It was the worst champagne he had ever tasted!'. The late William Swales of Lastingham (who lived until 1967) staked out the route, but the scheme got no further, it was rumoured Pope had absconded because little more was ever heard of it.

That a further railway should have been contemplated at this period is remarkable, as the population was declining and ironstone production long past its prime. Possibly the scenic attractions of the dale and district was the snare, visitors were increasing rapidly, almost every farm took guests or provided bed and breakfast.

The abandoned line provides a splendid route for the walker through the heart of the North York Moors with countless viewpoints at which to linger. Having undertaken such an excursion the visitor will readily understand the natural difficulties and isolation of the area penetrated by the Rosedale Branch over 100 years ago.

Thanks are due to Scarborough and District Archaeological Society for permission to quote extensively from Research Report No. 9 1974. 'Rosedale Mines and Railway' by R. H. Hayes and J. G. Rutter.

XX
The Dale

From Seven Stone, the source of the river, to Hartoft End, Rosedale stretches for eight miles. It continues another two miles to Beck House where it enters the limestone. The width varies from one and a quarter miles from Thorgill to Clough House, to less than half a mile at Hartoft End, where the moors come down to the stream on the west side. The scenery varies accordingly from heather moor and bogs, vivid with cotton-grass in mid-summer, to rocky defiles, wooded gorges, and 'holmes', or water meadows. In August-September, the masses of purple heather are a delight to see, especially from Bank Top, the Knott, or Hamer Road. Every season brings colour, even in the depth of winter the russet brown bracken contrasts with the dark heather, and craggy dalesides. After snow, a clear day brings a really Norwegian landscape, an unforgettable sight, though travellers are wise not to attempt the Castleton-Ralph Cross route, as drifting snow piles up to fantastic depths on the open moors.

The scars of the mining era have almost vanished but the ruined kilns, chimneys and abandoned railway track remain, to interest industrial archaeology enthusiasts.

Rosedale Abbey has returned to its former pastoral beauty, with many trees, green fields, and streams, surrounded by the mellow stonework of its dwellings.

There are several paths, pleasant walks over old pannier trods, one leads from the village by the fields over White Bridge, to Thorgill. Here is magnificent wild scenery, the narrow gill is fringed by steep grassy slopes leading to crags on the moor edge. Thorgill had only a few houses until mining times, when most were built and it is only a small hamlet today. The pannier trod up Daleside road can be followed to the converging tracks below Blakey. Another path from the village goes by Waterhouse Well (erroneously called 'Monk's Well') to Dunn Carr Bridge, where tracks divide

A general view of the East Mines about 1900. Notice the three levels of track, the loading gantries and metal trucks. The track bed of the various levels and the remains of cottages and kilns are still clearly visible.